. . . and these thy gifts

Gift of the SON

by

Richard Reichert

and

Sara Reichert

OUR SUNDAY VISITOR, INC.
Huntington, Indiana

Editorial Director: William Odell
Consultant: Edward J. Murray

Nihil Obstat: Rev. Richard P. Hire
Censor Librorum

Imprimatur: William McManus, D.D.
Bishop of Fort Wayne-South Bend
December 2, 1983

ISBN 0-87973-043-9

Published, printed, and bound in the United States of America by
Our Sunday Visitor, Inc.
200 Noll Plaza
Huntington, Indiana 46750

043

ACKNOWLEDGMENTS

Scripture texts used in this work are taken from the *New American Bible*, © 1970, and the Lectionary for Mass, © 1970 Confraternity of Christian Doctrine, Washington, D.C., and are used by license of said copyright owner. No part of the *New American Bible* may be reproduced in any form without permission in writing from the copyright owner. All rights reserved.

Excerpts from the English translation of the Order of Mass, © 1969 International Committee on English in the Liturgy, Inc. All rights reserved.

Cover design by Marcella Keller
Book design, art, and mechanicals by John D. Firestone & Associates, Inc., and James E. McIlrath.

Photo Credits: John D. Firestone & Associates, Inc. — pages viii, 5, 15b, 24, 35, 45, 46, 50, 55, 56, 63, 73, 80, 86, 92, 100, 104, 111, 113, 119, 120, 135, 140, 143, 144, 147, 148, 157, 170, and 174; Religious News Service — pages 15a, 16, 106, 134, 136, 169; John Zierten — pages 30, 42, 47, 52, 61, 68, 90, 94, 95, 105, 107, 124, 154, 160, 163, 172, 179, 180; Diane Garnette — pages 49, 70, 88, 93, 121, 125, 126; Richard Beemer — page 28; OSV File Photos — pages 12, 64, 97, 110, 131, 137, 150, 159, 176.

Contents

Unit 1 The Gospels: How They Came to Be

Unit 2 Ministry, Message, and Miracles

Unit 3 Followers, Faith, and the Future

Unit 4 No Greater Love

Unit 5 Beyond Pentecost

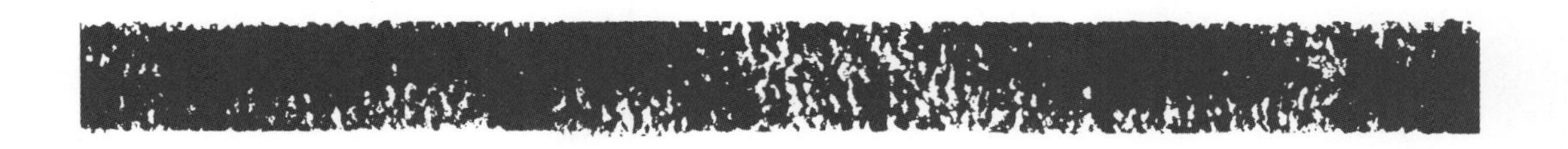

Dear Seventh-Grade Students,

Welcome to the seventh grade. It will be an important year for you in many ways. Your childhood will soon be a memory. The exciting and sometimes confusing teen years are near. So this is a good time to lay foundations and build friendships that can carry you through your teen years and into adulthood.

This course, we believe, can be a real help. It can help you discover Jesus in a new, more mature way — not just as your Savior, but as your friend. He is willing to to travel by your side, throughout your teen years, to guide, to encourage, to listen, and to help. All Jesus needs is your invitation to be your friend. May this text aid you in growing — and in becoming lifelong friends with Jesus.

Sincerely,

Richard Reichert

Sara Reichert

UNIT 1

The Gospels: How They Came to Be

INTRODUCTION

In this unit we will see how the Gospels came to be. Actually it was a somewhat long and involved process. They went through several stages of development before they reached the form we have today.

Gospel means "good news." The good news the Gospels contain is the good news of Jesus' resurrection. That's the key message of the Gospels. Everything else in the Gospels takes its meaning from that message.

Finally, as we'll see, the Gospels are "faith histories." The authors of the Gospels wrote what they had come to *believe* about Jesus, who he is, what he said and what he did. They certainly contain history. But the Gospels are not history books. They are faith accounts of historical events.

Since this first unit lays foundations for much of what follows in other units, you will want to study it carefully.

Jesus of Nazareth, Then and Now

"Is this not the carpenter, the son of Mary, a brother of James and Joses and Judas and Simon? Are not his sisters our neighbors here?" They found him too much for them.
(Mark 6.3)

A few years back the Beatles were still together as a group. They were at the peak of their popularity. This prompted one of them to remark that they were better known in their time than Jesus was in his time. That may sound like bragging but it was actually true.

Where's Galilee?

Jesus was born in Palestine, a small backwater country in the huge Roman Empire. He was a Jew. Jews weren't too well liked by the Romans or by other nations in the empire. Nobody outside the country would have paid much attention to Jesus. Even in Palestine, however, Jesus had a strike against him. He was a Galilean Jew. Galilee had a bad reputation as being backward, ignorant, and not too religious. Galileans were generally considered "hicks" by other Jews. They even spoke with a funny accent, a kind of twang that gave them away as Galileans wherever they went. They weren't very popular outside Galilee.

An Ordinary Man

Today, we are well aware of the miracle that surrounded Mary's conception of Jesus, but that was not common knowledge at the time. As he grew, Jesus learned to read and probably to write, but there is no record of any formal education. He was trained by his foster-father, Joseph, to be a carpenter, so he was sometimes called the carpenter's son. It was a working-class trade, which, like the rest of Jesus' early life, attracted little attention.

Though Jesus traveled throughout his homeland, he never went more than one hundred and fifty miles from the place of his birth. The largest city he ever visited was Jerusalem. It wasn't much if compared to Rome or other great centers of civilization in his time.

A Short Public Life

At about age thirty Jesus began to preach, much in the fashion of the wandering preachers of his time. He did enjoy some popularity for a while, especially with the lower classes. He gained something of a reputation as a healer and wonder worker. But from the start he angered the religious and civic leaders of the country. Gradually Jesus' popularity began to sag except for a rather small band of faithful followers. They were a slice of life from the common man — most all were uneducated, some were solid types like the Apostles, and many were lower-class and even outcast types.

The religious leaders succeeded in having him condemned to death after only three short years of preaching because they feared he was ruining the Jewish religion.

He was executed by crucifixion, a very cruel death used for the worst kinds of criminals. After his arrest, which was aided by one of his own followers, most of the others left him out of fear for their own lives. At his death only his mother, a few other women and one of his disciples remained by him. By all human reason that should have been the end of the story.

The Faith of Billions

Two thousand years later one out of every three people alive is counted as a follower of Jesus. His story, the New Testament, has been told in every part of the world. It has been translated into almost every existing language. Countless people have willingly died rather than betray their faith in him. His followers over the centuries have dedicated their whole lives to the work Jesus began. They have made his teaching on brotherly love for the poor, the sick, and the outcasts a reality.

Keep in mind, however, Jesus didn't simply begin by starting a new religion. He first aim was to perfect the teaching that had been handed down through the Jewish religion for centuries. Only towards the end of his public ministry did it become clear that he intended to form a Church with Peter as its "rock." Aside from that, he never wrote a book, led a conquering army, or took control of any government. He spent his whole life mostly with the poor of society.

Who Is This Man?

Yet historians consider Jesus the single most important person in the history of the world. He has influenced more people and the course of history more dramatically than anyone else. His influence continues to grow two thousand years after he was executed as though he were a criminal. How do we account for this, given his background, the limited amount of time he was in the public eye (three years), and the reason for and manner of his death?

For us today, with our faith, the answer is easy. He is the Son of God! But even his followers in his own time weren't so ready to admit that. At least not at first. So if we look to the starting point for Jesus' influence and following over the centuries we must look to one event — his resurrection! We'll do that in the next chapter.

What Has This Got to Do With Me?

Have you ever been rejected or put down because you are too short, too tall, too fat, too thin, "dumb," or not "cool," because of your race, color, or the family you are from? Do you think Jesus could understand how you felt?

Do you ever expect to be really famous, say like the Beatles? Do you think you could still make a difference if you never become famous?

Have you ever had a nickname you didn't like? Do you think Jesus, the Nazarene, could understand how you felt?

DID YOU KNOW?

What's in a Name?

Jesus is the Greek version of the Hebrew name Joshua. It means "Yahweh is salvation." It was a fairly common name. Jesus was often referred to as "the Nazarene" by Jews of his time because he grew up in Nazareth, a small town in Galilee. It apparently had a bad reputation because there was a popular saying in Jesus' time "Can anything good come out of Nazareth?" We don't know just why it had such a bad reputation.

In Jesus' time most people didn't have last names or family names like we do today. Men were simply referred to as "the son of . . ." and their town. The Hebrew word for "son of" was "bar." So Jesus was probably sometimes called Jesus bar Joseph of Nazareth.

When Pilate put the title over Jesus' cross at his death, "Jesus of Nazareth, King of the Jews," it was intended as a double insult to the Jewish leaders. It was bad enough to suggest that a condemned man was King of the Jews, but it was even worse to suggest that someone from Nazareth of Galilee could be the Jewish king.

Review Questions and Activities

1. Name three things Jesus had against him when he started to preach.
2. Try to find out how many Christians (followers of Jesus) live in your town or city.
3. How long ago did Jesus live? Where? What was the ruling power?
4. Why were the Jewish leaders so angry at Pilate's sign over Jesus' cross?
5. What does the name Jesus mean?

Scripture Focus

- *Mark 6.3*

CHAPTER 2

Resurrection: The Event That Changed History

If there is no resurrection of the dead, Christ himself has not been raised. And if Christ has not been raised, our preaching is void of content and your faith is empty too.
(1 Corinthians 15.13-14)

When you read the four resurrection accounts in the Gospels there are a few things you notice. First, each account is a little different. They don't always agree on the times when Jesus appeared or to whom he appeared, but they all do agree that Jesus did reappear, alive, resurrected! A few other things they agree on are these:

• There were no eyewitnesses present at the exact moment when Jesus came from the tomb.

• There was a lot of mixed emotion in each account, fear, joy, confusion.

• There was some initial disbelief that Jesus was really alive.

• When Jesus did appear, some of his followers didn't recognize him at first.

Take time now to read the four Gospel accounts. You will find them in Matthew 28; Mark 16; Luke 24 and John 20-21.

What a Surprise

What are we to make of these stories? First, it's obvious that the followers of Jesus were taken completely by surprise. Even though Jesus had told them at various times that he would die and rise again, they didn't understand what he meant. So when he did suddenly appear to them they were taken off guard. That can explain their initial disbelief, and the fear and confusion that was mixed with their joy.

Secondly, Jesus was different in his resurrected state. That's probably why they didn't recognize him at first. Sure, they could see him, touch him and hear him. He wasn't some cloud of white smoke that we see in movies about ghosts. He was real. He could eat with them. He even cooked a meal for them. Yet he was different from what he was

before his death. He could appear and disappear at will. Walls and locked doors were no problem to him. Though the Gospels don't say so directly, it was as if Jesus' body had gained a spiritual quality. The laws of nature, like gravity and weight and time, no longer applied to Jesus' body. The Apostle Paul, in a letter to the Corinthians, described the resurrected body in this way:

> *When you sow, you do not sow a full-blown plant, but a kernel of wheat or some other grain. . . . So it is with the resurrection of the dead. What is sown in the earth is subject to decay, what rises is incorruptible. What is sown is ignoble, what rises is glorious. Weakness is sown, strength rises up. A natural body is put down and a spiritual body comes up.*
>
> *(1 Corinthians 15.37, 42-44)*

In other words Paul compares our earthly body — and Jesus' — to a seed. After a seed is buried in the soil it is transformed into something new — a living, vital plant. Our earthly body is prone to sickness, disease, suffering and death. Our resurrected body — like Jesus' resurrected body — will be glorious and no longer have the limits our earthly body has. So Jesus didn't simply "come back to life." He was resurrected, transformed, glorified.

Resurrection Is Different

Frequently, we hear about some heart-attack victim or drowning victim who had apparently died but was brought back to life by CPR (cardiopulmonary resuscitation) or other medical help. These people had apparently died in the sense that the heart stopped beating, the lungs stopped working and they were unconscious. Some have remained in that state ten minutes or longer before they were "brought back to life." But note what being "brought back to life" means here. It means a person regains consciousness; it means the heart starts beating again and the lungs start working. The person is just the way he or she was before the accident. The body didn't change in

Spiritual Body in Life After Life	Risen Body of Jesus
1. Sees others, but is unseen by others.	**1.** Sees others, but is seen only by his followers, who don't immediately recognize him.
2. Outside the physical body, but senses what is being done to the body.	**2.** The physical body, which died and was buried, is changed into a combination spiritual and physical body.
3. Movement is quick and effortless.	**3.** Jesus can suddenly appear and disappear.
4. Can pass through physical objects.	**4.** Can pass through physical objects.
5. Cannot be touched.	**5.** Can be touched.
6. Shape of this body is uncertain, not easily described.	**6.** Eats, drinks, and talks with his followers.
7. Returns to the physical body to resume life as before.	**7.** Ascends to his Father.

Notice the similarities and differences in life after life, as described by Dr. Raymond Moody, and the risen body of Jesus, as described in the Gospel.

any way. The person has the same limits and powers (certainly no greater powers) as before the accident. Most important of all, however, the person must still face death at some future time.

But that isn't how it was with Jesus. Jesus wasn't simply brought back to life. He was resurrected and his body was transformed! He had conquered death, not simply slipped away from death. He now lives in his resurrected body, a body that is beyond death and suffering.

That makes Jesus' resurrection the event that changed history. Many people have been brought back to life for a time, but no one else, before or since, has ever experienced such a transforming resurrection.

It Begins to Make Sense

We can be sure the Apostles were overjoyed once they became convinced that Jesus was back with them. But the turning point was when they finally began to understand what Jesus' resurrection really meant.

It meant that through Jesus all people could one day enjoy the same kind of resurrection. Death of the physical body need no longer be feared as the end of all. In fact, it is just the beginning of true, perfect life. Gradually the real meaning of what Jesus taught them began to dawn on them. Jesus said things like, "Whoever believes in me shall never die." After experiencing the resurrected Jesus, the Jesus who conquered death, the Apostles got a whole new meaning from those words. So when Jesus gave them the final command to go and to teach all nations, they knew exactly what to teach: They taught the good news that Jesus had died but is now resurrected. They taught that all people can enjoy eternal, resurrected life through Jesus. Now that was good news! It is this belief in the resurrected Jesus that has changed all history.

Another Version

But not everyone believes Jesus was really resurrected. We saw in Matthew's resurrection account how the religious leaders arranged to spread rumors that Jesus' followers had simply stolen his body and then made up the story of his resurrection. Some people of that day probably accepted those rumors as the truth.

Throughout history there have been other kinds of attempts to explain away the resurrection. Some have argued that Jesus never really died on the cross. He merely passed out or went into a kind of coma. When he was placed in the cool tomb and allowed to rest he recovered and then left the tomb. Some have argued that Jesus never appeared to his followers, but that they experienced a kind of group hypnosis or group hallucination. Some have even tried to make Jesus' death and resurrection into a fantastic plot cooked up by Jesus himself. They say that Jesus and the soldiers were in it together. They were to fake Jesus' death so that when he reappeared Jesus could say he had returned from death and gain new followers.

As True Today

We can see not everyone is willing to accept the message the Apostles preached. But preach it they did, and with such conviction and belief in Jesus' resurrection that each accepted martyrdom. Two thousand years later the followers of Jesus still preach the same message. Jesus is risen. Jesus has conquered sin and death. Jesus is Lord! History has never been the same since that first Easter morning.

What Has This Got to Do With Me?

Does Jesus' resurrection affect the way you feel about death?

How would your own life be different if Jesus had never appeared to his followers?

What does it mean for you to be a follower of the resurrected Jesus?

DID YOU KNOW?

Shroud of Turin

The Shroud of Turin is probably the most studied piece of cloth in history. It is a burial cloth of the kind used in Palestine around the first century. On it is both the front and back image of a man about five feet eight inches tall, with a full beard and shoulder-length hair. He is well proportioned and appears to be in his mid-thirties at the time of his burial. The image shows signs of wounds: nail holes in the wrists and feet, wounds from a very brutal whipping over most of the body, but especially the back and legs, pierce marks around the head. Finally there is a lance wound in the side. In other words, the image is of a person who had been scourged, crowned with thorns, and then crucified exactly as described in the Gospels.

Even today, using space-age science, no one can explain how the image came to be. It is not painted on the cloth. The blood stains are of real blood. The cloth itself is ancient and contains pollen of the type found in first century Palestine.

Is it the burial cloth of Jesus? Is it Jesus' face that appears on it? We may never know for certain but, more and more, the evidence suggests an answer of "yes." Scientists continue to study it.

See the image of his face on p. 12.

Review Questions and Activities

1. What is the difference between being resurrected and being brought back to life?
2. Why do you think the Apostles weren't able to recognize Jesus at first?
3. How can you explain the Apostles' initial disbelief?
4. What was the key message the Apostles began to preach?
5. How did the religious leaders try to deal with Jesus' resurrection?

Scripture Focus

- *1 Corinthians 15.13-14*

New Testament Background: The Old Testament

Therefore let the whole house of Israel know beyond any doubt that God has made both Lord and Messiah this Jesus whom you crucified.

(Acts 2.36)

Jesus was a devout Jew. Like any devout Jew of his time, he was very familiar with the history of his people and with the Scriptures, which told their story. That history began with Abraham, the father of faith and the father of the Jewish people. All devout Jews considered themselves sons and daughters of Abraham.

Kingdom = A Land

Through Abraham, the Jewish people first entered into a covenant or special relationship with God. Through Abraham, God had promised the Jews a special land. It was that very land where Jesus now lived, even though it had been conquered many times by foreign rulers. Because it was the promised holy land of Abraham and their ancestors, the Jews of Jesus' time were still willing to fight and even to die, if necessary, to keep it as their own.

All good Jews also knew how God had rescued their ancestors from Egypt and how, through Moses, he gave them the Law in the desert. Each year at Passover they would recall and celebrate that event. All year long they would study and seek to obey the Law of Moses.

A very important part of Jewish history was the conquest of the Promised Land and the establishment of their religious kingdom. Jews looked back to the time of David and Solomon as a kind of high point in their history — when Israel was rich and powerful.

But they also could recall that the kingdom of David and Solomon soon collapsed, first from civil war and then from outside invaders. From then on it was a long, sad story of foreign invaders, captivity, and even the destruction of Jerusalem and Solomon's temple.

A Messiah Is Promised

One very important thing took place in the time of David which continued to give the Jews hope through all the bad times, right up to the time of Jesus. God had made a special promise to David: one of his descendants would become king and would reestablish the kingdom. There would be peace, prosperity, and honor in Israel once again. Justice would reign. This hope for a king like David came to be called messianism. The people looked for a Messiah who would come and lead them. (Messiah is Hebrew for "anointed." The Messiah would be God's specially chosen and anointed one. "Christ" is the Greek word for anointed or Messiah, by the way.)

This hope for a Messiah was kept alive and was developed by most of the great prophets. Jeremiah spoke about it. Isaiah probably spoke about it the most. We get some of the most famous passages about the coming Messiah from him. Ezekiel spoke about a Messiah. So did Daniel. Many of the Psalms have the Messiah as a key theme. Much of the Old Testament from the time of David onward spoke about the coming Messiah.

Joined with the theme of Messiah in the Old Testament was the theme of a renewed and perfect covenant. The Jews had broken the Covenant of Moses many times and were often punished by God for it. But the prophets talked about a time when God would forgive them once and for all and establish a new, perfect covenant that would last forever.

In Jesus' Time

A new kingdom, a new leader (or Messiah), and a renewed, perfect covenant were three things that the Jews longed for and hoped for. This longing and hope were especially strong by the time of Jesus.

Israel was once more a conquered people living under pagan rule. Their present king, Herod, was not a religious person. He openly broke the Covenant laws. In Jesus' day there was much talk that the time had finally come. Any day now the Messiah would appear. It was a major theme of most of the preachers who wandered about the land.

If this is so, why didn't the people recognize Jesus as the promised Messiah when he appeared on the scene? Didn't he preach about the coming of the kingdom and about a renewed covenant? Wasn't he a descendant of David's family, the family of kings?

For one thing, the people had come to look for a powerful, worldly Messiah, one who would lead them to war and victory against the hated Romans. Jesus preached peace and forgiveness of enemies — hardly the stuff of revolutions and victories over enemy armies. For another thing, Jesus was a Galilean, from Nazareth, from a humble background — hardly the stuff kings are made of. Finally, Jesus' preaching went against the teaching of the religious leaders of the day. He accused them of leading the people astray. This didn't make him very popular with them. In fact, that's why they had him killed.

We can look back now and see how well Jesus actually fulfilled the messianic prophecies of the Old Testament. To most people of his day, though, it didn't seem that way. A great teacher, yes. A wonder worker and holy

The Wailing Wall is part of the old Temple.

person, yes, maybe even a prophet, but not the Messiah. Jesus' closest followers became pretty sure that he was the Messiah. But they still had their doubts until after his resurrection.

Jesus: A Man With Roots

Old Testament history, the escape from Egypt, the establishment of the Covenant, the establishment of the kingdom, the messianic hope: That's the background we need to approach the life and teaching of Jesus. He was a Jew, speaking to Jews. He always made references to the Old Testament. He used the Psalms and prophecies about the messiah, the new kingdom and New Covenant. Even if the Jews of his time didn't believe him, they, at least, were familiar with what he was talking about.

That was certainly Peter's approach when he began his own preaching on Pentecost. Listen to what he tells the people:

> *Brothers, I can speak confidently to you about our father David. He died and was buried, and his grave is in our midst to this day. He was a prophet and knew that God had sworn to him that one of his descendants would sit upon his throne. He said that he was not abandoned to the nether world, nor did his body undergo corruption, thus proclaiming beforehand the resurrection of the Messiah. This is the Jesus God has raised up, and we are witnesses. . . . Therefore let the whole house of Israel know beyond any doubt that God has made both Lord and Messiah this Jesus whom you crucified.*
>
> (Acts 2.29-32,36)

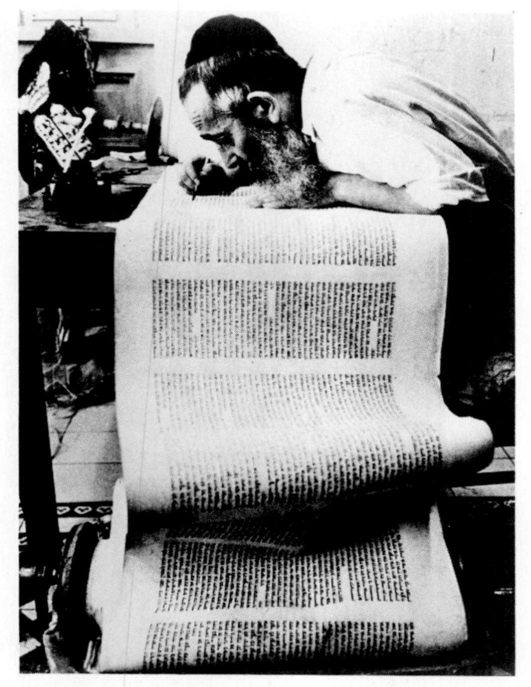

A scroll of the Hebrew Scriptures.

Peter knew his audience would be familiar with David, the promises God made to him, the prophecies about the Messiah. He simply showed that in the *risen Jesus* all these promises and prophecies were fulfilled.

In Jesus the Old Covenant gives way to a New Covenant. A new kingdom of peace and justice is established and the risen Jesus is its king.

What Has This Got to Do With Me?

Does the belief that "Jesus will come again" change your life in any way?

What does Jesus' New Covenant mean to you? What should it mean?

Should you be looking for God's kingdom? What is God's kingdom?

DID YOU KNOW?

What the Prophets Said

Here are a few of the more famous prophecies regarding the Messiah that are found in the Old Testament. Look them up.

- Where the Messiah would be born: Micah 5.1-2.
- When the Messiah would be born: Daniel 9.
- His virgin birth: Isaiah 7.14.
- His herald: Isaiah 40.3-5; Malachi 3.1.
- His reign and other qualities: Isaiah 9.1-6.
- His suffering and resurrection: Isaiah 50.1-4; 52.13-15; 53; Psalm 16; Psalm 22.

Review Questions and Activities

1. When did messianism begin?
2. Besides messianism, what kept the Jews' hopes alive in hard times?
3. What are some reasons the people of his time didn't think Jesus was the Messiah?
4. When did Jesus' followers finally become convinced that he was indeed the awaited Messiah?

Scripture Focus

- *Acts 2.36*

Old Testament Landmark Dates

1750-1300 B.C. Age of the Patriarchs

The call of Abraham; birth of Isaac, Jacob and Esau; Jacob's twelve sons (Twelve tribes of Israel); Joseph rules in Egypt and the Israelites move there. Israelites held captive in Egypt and reduced to slavery.

1300-1200 B.C. Passover-Exodus-Covenant Experience

Moses becomes leader; God saves his people from Egypt; the desert and the Covenant experience; receiving of the Ten Commandments.

1200-1020 B.C. Conquest of the Promised Land

Israelites gradually conquer the Promised Land, divide it among the twelve tribes and settle down. Led by famous Judges.

1020-922 B.C. The Kingdom and the Temple

Period of the beginning of the kingdom; kingships of Saul, David and Solomon; the Temple is built. Peak of the kingdom; beginning of messianism.

922-722 B.C. The Kingdom Is Divided, Declines

Civil wars between northern and southern tribes; foreign powers invade periodically. Time of the prophets Elijah, Elisha, Hosea and Amos. Assyria conquers the northern kingdom and forces the people to leave their homeland.

722-597 B.C. Southern Kingdom, Judah, Falls Into Evil Ways

Prophet Isaiah starts messianic movement. He prepares the people for the Messiah's arrival.

597-538 B.C. Babylonian Captivity

Southern kingdom is conquered by Babylon and led into captivity in Babylonia. Jerusalem and the Temple are destroyed. Isaiah and Jeremiah preaches before the captivity; Ezekiel preaches in Babylonia; messianism grows stronger.

538-428 B.C. Jerusalem and Temple Rebuilt

Israelites return to their homeland and rebuild. It is a period of religious reform. Time of Nehemiah, Ezra.

428-63 B.C. Foreign Rulers

A series of foreign powers conquer and rule the Jews. These include the Persians, the Greeks, the Egyptians, the Syrians, and finally, in 63 B.C. the Romans. Time of Alexander the Great. During the Syrian rule, the famous Maccabean revolt takes place. Messianism grows stronger until it peaks about the time of Jesus.

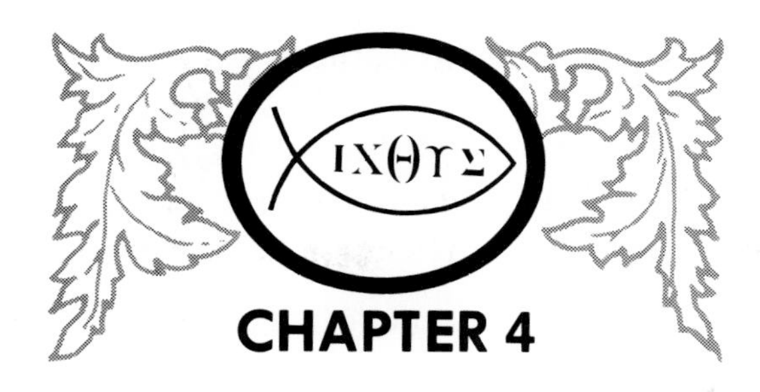

New Testament Background: Life at the Time of Jesus

The LORD then said to him, "This is the land which I swore to Abraham, Isaac and Jacob that I would give to their descendants. I have let you feast your eyes upon it, but you shall not cross over."
(Deuteronomy 34.4)

We saw in the last chapter that it helps us understand Jesus' life and teaching if we know some Old Testament history. It gives us clues about what influenced him and the people around him.

It's just as important to know something about the country in which Jesus lived all his life and about the people with whom he lived. In faith we know that Jesus is the Son of God, that he is divine. In faith we also know Jesus is fully human and "like us in all things except sin." This means he had to learn to crawl and to walk just as we did. He had to learn to speak as we did. The language he learned was that of the people around him. He ate the food of his people. He played the games popular with his playmates. He worked alongside his people. We know that where a person grows up and lives has a lot to do with how a person thinks, what the person values, how that person acts.

Where You Live Shapes Who You Are

Eskimos in the Arctic region think and act quite differently from people living in the desert regions of North Africa or in the jungle regions along the Amazon of South America. The same is true for Jesus, the man. Jesus was a Jew. He was raised a Jew and spent his life with Jews. He lived all his life in Palestine, a country about one hundred and fifty miles long and about fifty-five miles across at its widest part. This country was on the eastern coast of the Mediterranean Sea. It was between Egypt to the south and Syria and Persia to the north and west. It was a kind of crossroads in the Mideast. It was a popular path for caravans — and for armies. That's why so many countries

Palestine in the north.

tried to control it over the centuries. Controlling it gave them some control over the whole area.

In Jesus' time, as we know, the Romans controlled it. It still remained a popular route for caravans and travelers. Even if Jesus never traveled more than one hundred and fifty miles from his birthplace, he had many opportunities to see and to experience people and cultures from around the known world. Jews lived not only in Israel but throughout the world at that time. Many would make a pilgrimage to Jerusalem and the Temple to celebrate Passover or some other feast. For example, look at the list of peoples who were in Jerusalem when Peter gave his first speech on Pentecost, a Jewish feast: "How is it that each of us hears them in his native tongue? We are Parthians, Medes and Elamites. We live in Mesopotamia, Judea and Cappadocia, Pontus, the province of Asia, Phrygia and Pamphylia, Egypt and the regions of Libya and Cyrene. There are even visitors from Rome . . . Cretans and Arabs too" (Acts 2.8-11).

Jesus was a Jew, but he had contact with the rest of the known world as he grew up and when he preached.

A Geographical Grab Bag

Ancient Palestine or present-day Israel is a real mix of geography. Yet it is no larger than the state of Vermont. To the north, or the region of Galilee, there are rolling hills, rich farm lands, lush vegetation and one of the most beautiful and fruitful lakes in the world, the Sea of Galilee. At the southern end of the same country we have mountains and desert regions where nothing grows — and the Dead Sea, so salt-filled that *nothing* can live in it. The southern region was called

Palestine in the south.

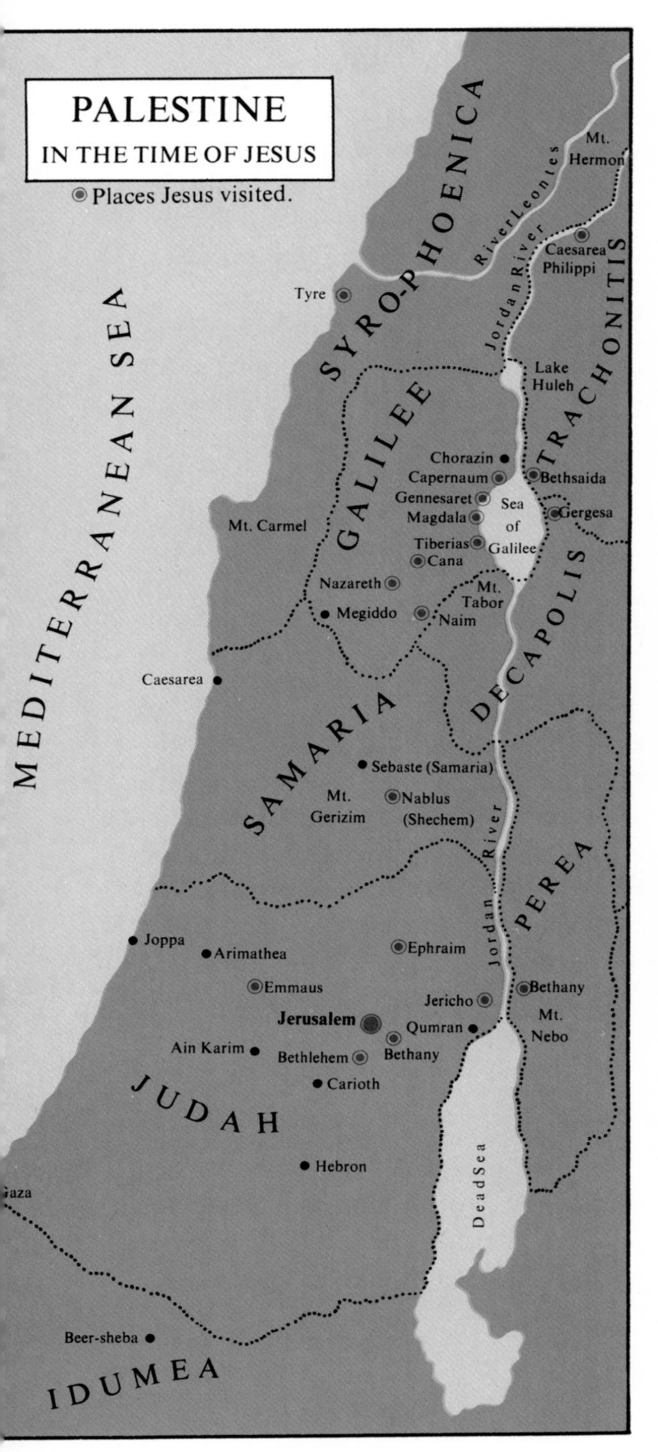

Judea at the time. Jerusalem was there, sitting on the mountainsides. Hence the saying, "Let us go up to Jerusalem." It was an uphill climb from anywhere in the country.

Between Galilee and Judea was Samaria, a hilly region. Jews hated Samaritans. The Samaritans felt the same way about Jews. Both were descendants of Abraham but they approached their religion differently. Their hatred goes all the way back to the time of the civil wars after the death of Solomon. When traveling from Judea to Galilee, good Jews would even go miles out of their way to avoid traveling through Samaria. That's why Jesus' parable of the Good Samaritan was such a blow to his listeners. That Jesus even suggested there could be such a thing as a "good" Samaritan was an insult to the Jews of his time.

Running through most of the length of the country was the Jordan River. It flowed south, connecting the Sea of Galilee with the Dead Sea. Part of the Jordan River valley was good for farming, but part was not, as the river also ran through desert regions, especially as it neared the Dead Sea. It was in such a desert region that Jesus went to be baptized by John.

The climate of the country was mostly mild to just plain hot, especially in the summer and in desert regions. In the winter, or rainy season, it could get cold and in the higher areas it would even snow on occasion.

Jesus Was In Touch

In his life, Jesus traveled to every part of his country. He experienced all its nice places and its ugly places. He walked steep mountain roads, crossed desert regions, sat by the shore of the Sea of Galilee. He crossed farmers' fields, the pasture land where sheep grazed, and the Sea of Galilee on a boat. He ate in the homes of poor people and of rich merchants. He visited little villages, like his own village of Nazareth. He taught in the Temple and the crowded streets of Jerusalem, a city of about 150,000 people (many more when the pilgrims came for feast days).

He was at home with every class of people who lived in his country: farmers and shepherds, fishermen and merchants, soldiers and priests, prostitutes and tax collectors, learned scholars and outcast lepers, craftsmen and beggars. Most people in his time were poor in terms of money and possessions. As is often the case, the number of the rich and powerful, religious and political leaders, was rather small, and they were in charge.

There was a big gap between the wealthy ruling class and the vast majority who were poor and oppressed. But all good Jews felt the same about two things. All of them hated the Roman invaders. All of them shared a devotion to their religion and to the Temple.

Some Groups

The Jews loved their religion and their Temple. But there were some important parties or groups who did not always agree with one another. Jesus had to deal with all of them. They included:

• *Pharisees:* (Means separated one.) They are best known for urging a strict following of the Law, to which they added many other regulations, which were later written down in a famous book called the Talmud. Some Pharisees were very sincere, but Jesus accused many of them of being hypocrites who made it more difficult for people to obey the Covenant. St. Paul was once a Pharisee. Most of them were laymen, not priests.

• *Sadducees:* (From Sadoc, a priest at the time of David.) Most of these were members of the priestly family. They were part of the ruling class and encouraged others to cooperate with Rome rather than revolt. They controlled the Sanhedrin or the Jewish ruling body of the time. They disagreed with the Pharisees about some religious issues like resurrection.

• *Scribes:* These were men learned in the Law. People looked to them to help them interpret the Law. Some scribes were Pharisees, some Sadducees.

• *Zealots:* This was a political group more than a religious group. They sought to drive the Romans out by

force and were opposed to any cooperation or compromise with the Romans. Simon, one of Jesus' chosen Apostles, was a Zealot. This party eventually led the great revolt in A.D. 70 which resulted in the destruction of Jerusalem by the Romans.

• *Essenes:* Every other group in this list is mentioned in the Gospels. This one is not. The Essenes were a very religious sect who lived much like monks of today, in communities apart from the rest of the people. They followed the Law as perfectly as they could and tried to avoid all contact with whatever the Law declared unclean. They performed many ritual washings each day. One of their key beliefs was that a messiah would come very soon. They had a monastery at Qumran which is not far from where John the Baptizer preached and where Jesus was baptized.

• *Priests:* In the Jewish religion a person was a priest because he was born of the priestly family or tribe. They were given certain special privileges and took turns performing sacrifices and other duties at the Temple. Some priests were Pharisees, but most belonged to the Sadducee group.

Here are a few other classes of people, not religious groups, which were important in the time of Jesus for various reasons.

• *Publicans:* These were tax collectors who worked for the Romans. The Jews

hated them. If a Jew took that position he was doubly hated as a traitor. They got paid a percentage of what they collected so it was in their interest to get as much tax money as they could in any way that they could. The Apostle Matthew was once a tax collector. Many Jews were angry at Jesus because he associated with publicans.

• *Lepers:* In Jesus' time any person with a skin disease thought to be contagious was called a leper. It didn't mean just those with real leprosy. A person with a skin rash or chicken pox would be considered a leper and had to stay away from people and public places until he or she could prove that the disease was cured. For real lepers this meant the rest of their lives. They were even expected to carry a bell and ring it to warn people not to come near them. Perhaps the worst part for devout Jews with such diseases was that they couldn't go to the Temple or synagogue. Jesus, of course, associated with lepers and often cured them.

• *Rabbis:* (Means teacher.) These were persons who had a reputation for being learned in the Law. Usually they led the services in the synagogue and answered questions the people would ask. They didn't need any special training and didn't receive any pay as such. Jesus was called rabbi by the people. In the Jewish religion today the position of rabbi is an official position and requires special training. Today a rabbi has a role much like the parish priest in the Catholic religion.

And the Romans. . .

Jesus didn't just have to deal with the Jewish religious leaders. There were political leaders as well. The Romans were the official rulers. The emperor of the time appointed procurators to actually rule the country. Pontius Pilate was a procurator at the time of Jesus' death. The Romans still allowed the Jews to have their king (Herod, during Jesus' public ministry — not the same one who ruled when Jesus was born) and council like the Sanhedrin, but the real power stayed with the Romans. They had an army to back them up. Israel had no army at the time, nor was it allowed to have one. The Romans gave the Jews much religious freedom and didn't try to force them to worship the emperor or pagan gods. The Romans knew what happened when other conquerors had tried this. Trouble! But they did collect high taxes which were sent to Rome. In general, the Romans offended the Jews by being there and by bullying them around. It was the Romans, at the urging of the religious leaders, who finally executed Jesus — Roman style. The Roman rulers held the power of life and death over all the Jews, and didn't let them forget it.

All of these things — the geography and climate, the people and their customs, the religious groups and the political powers — influenced Jesus, his teaching style, and his ministry. The more you come to know about the place and time in which Jesus lived the better you will be able to understand the Gospels

What Has This Got to Do With Me?

How do you feel about the religious leaders of our times? How do they influence you?

What about your political leaders?

How much does knowing about Jesus' country and times help you understand how Jesus acted and how he felt?

DID YOU KNOW?

Life's Comforts

In Jesus' time the most common food of the poor was a coarse bread made from barley. Only wealthy people could afford bread made from wheat. Such bread was a rare treat for the poor. They used honey to sweeten food, not sugar. There weren't many cows so milk came mostly from sheep and goats. Eating meat or eggs was a luxury few poor people could afford except on special occasions. But fish, a good source of protein, was fairly plentiful and inexpensive. It was most often dried or smoked. Fresh fish was available only near the shores where it was caught because the hot climate made it spoil quickly. Vegetables like lentils, cucumbers, onions, and lettuce were plentiful, so were fruits and nuts like grapes, dates, olives, figs, melons, apricots, pomegranates, walnuts, almonds, and pistachios. People prepared food over open fires and in clay ovens. In places like Jerusalem smoke from cooking fires got so thick, open fires became outlawed. Wood could be hard to find and expensive. Water was also precious in many areas of the country, especially during the dry season. Wells played an important part in the social life of the women, who had to gather there each day to get the day's supply. Houses of the poor were made mostly from field stones packed with mud, which dried to a cementlike hardness. Roofs were made from reeds mixed with clay. These had to be replaced regularly. There was no indoor plumbing, of course.

In short, life for most people in the time of Jesus was a tough, daily struggle, with few real comforts or luxuries. Jesus grew and lived with such people.

Review Questions and Activities

1. How big was Israel in Jesus' time?
2. Who controlled Israel in Jesus' time?
3. Why did the Jews hate the Samaritans?
4. What were the major religious groups in Jesus' time?
5. What river ran through Israel and what two seas did it connect?

Scripture Focus

- *Deuteronomy 34.4*

The New Testament Begins: Oral Tradition

Day after day, both in the temple and at home, they never stopped teaching and proclaiming the good news of Jesus the Messiah.
(Acts 5.42)

The New Testament as we have it today didn't just happen overnight. It was developed in several stages. The source for what it contains is Jesus' life, his deeds, and his words. It is important to remember, though, when Jesus was preaching and healing, his followers weren't going around taking careful notes on everything. They listened, they saw, they wondered about it — and often they didn't understand it.

Nobody Took Notes

It never occurred to Jesus' followers to keep a day-to-day record, noting dates and places and exact words. That's how it often is with people who become famous later on. For example, when Abraham Lincoln was growing up, he wasn't followed around by reporters or biographers who wrote down what he said and did. It was only much later, when he was president, and then after his death, that people wanted to know more about his childhood, what he was like, what he did and said. By that time, they had to depend upon the memories of people who had known him as a child. Such people remembered some things, but certainly not everything.

That's how it was with Jesus, not just as a child, but even when he started his public life. There were no accurate, day-to-day records, just the memories of his Apostles and other followers.

Listen to Me

That brings us to the second stage of the development of the New Testament: oral tradition. Oral tradition means that the Apostles began to preach about Jesus, based on what they remembered. Keep in mind one important fact here: when the Apostles began to preach about the words and deeds of Jesus they did so

"Street preacher" — the oral tradition is still alive.

after the resurrection. That is, they preached out of their own faith that Jesus was the Messiah.

Why is this important? Because it shaped what they remembered and what they said. Now that they believed Jesus was the Messiah, much of what he had said and done took on new meaning. When they recalled Jesus' teachings and actions, they would often add the new meaning to what he had said, even if Jesus hadn't said it in quite that way. But we'll get back to that.

Jesus Is Messiah

When the Apostles first began to preach they were talking mostly to Jews. They had a single purpose in mind: to convince the Jews that Jesus was the Messiah they were looking for. So the basic message they preached was Jesus' death and resurrection. Most people were aware of his death; they had to be convinced about his resurrection. Most people were familiar with the Old Testament passages about the Messiah; they had to be convinced that these passages were fulfilled by Jesus.

A good example of this basic preaching, the earliest preaching of the Apostles, can be found in Acts 2.14-41, when Peter talked to the crowd on Pentecost. Look it up and read it now.

The oldest oral tradition was the story of Jesus' death and resurrection. This was the main foundation for the later, written New Testament. There was only a small reference to Jesus healing people and teaching them. That was common knowledge to the people of the country.

Only gradually did the oral tradition grow to include most of Jesus' public life and then even some stories about his conception and birth and earliest years.

The Gospel Grows

Why did the oral tradition grow? For several reasons. First was the simple fact that only the Apostles — those "who had walked with Jesus from the beginning" of his public life — had *seen and heard* all that he had done and said. It would be natural for converts to want to know more and more about Jesus. They would ask the Apostles to tell them about Jesus, and the Apostles did.

Just as important, the Apostles wanted to teach the new followers what Jesus had taught them, so they could be faithful followers of Jesus. The Apostles would tell them how Jesus had taught them to forgive their enemies, to beware of false prophets, and about all Jesus had said concerning the kingdom of God.

Secondly, sometimes even as the Apostles spoke, they would suddenly understand better themselves what Jesus really meant. This was the Holy Spirit working in them, helping them remember, helping them understand, helping them teach. In other words the Holy Spirit inspired their teaching so they wouldn't mislead people or forget the important things.

A third reason oral tradition kept developing was that as new problems arose, the converts would come to the Apostles to ask them what to do. Maybe the new followers wanted to know if they should pay taxes to Caesar, since Jesus was their real king. That would be a logical time for the Apostles to tell how Jesus had answered that question to the Pharisees (Mark 12.13-17).

Or perhaps some followers wanted to know why some of the people who first accepted Jesus as the Messiah turned away later when the Jewish officials mistreated them. That might be a time for telling Jesus' parable about the sower and the seed (Luke 8.4-15). The Apostles might even go on to explain what the parable meant in some detail. Their explanation would then become part of the oral tradition.

Then suppose one of the followers became sick. The community and the Apostles would go to the person to pray for him or her. They might recall one of the times when Jesus cured someone and tell that story to cheer up the sick person. The oral tradition grew some more. But the eucharistic meal was probably the one place where oral tradition grew most. Jesus gave his Apostles the command to remember him especially by celebrating the Last Supper together. "As often as you do these things, do them in memory of me."

Meals Were Special

It would be especially at eucharistic meals that the Apostles and disciples would tell their stories about Jesus, his words and deeds. What they focused on might depend on the kinds of problems the community had that day, the kinds of questions people asked, or needs they had. In short, the community not only retold the story of Jesus' death and resurrection at these meals — for that was what they were celebrating — but

We tell Jesus' story today in the liturgy of the Word at Mass.

they told various other stories about Jesus as well.

Since, in the early days of Christianity, all the followers were Jews, the Apostles would also read passages from the Old Testament as they used to do at synagogue services. Often they would choose passages that seemed to foretell or be similar to certain things that Jesus said and did.

That's basically how the Mass of today began: with a Last Supper type of meal recalling Jesus' death and resurrection; and with stories about Jesus — today's Scripture readings and homily.

Stories, Stories

In any case, the second stage in the development of the New Testament was based on oral tradition: these were stories about Jesus that were remembered and shaped according to the situation in which the Apostles found themselves. These were spoken stories.

There wasn't any real order to these stories. That is, they didn't start with the first thing Jesus said or the first thing he did and then go on to the next day in his life. Just as important, there were Twelve Apostles and any number of other disciples telling these stories to different people in different places for different reasons. No wonder there are several versions of the same story.

Let's Write It Down

Only gradually did it occur to people to begin to write down these stories. When they did, they usually did it with some logic or theme. For example, they would begin to make a collection of Jesus' teachings about the kingdom, or a collection of stories about his miracles, or a collection of stories about the parables he told. There would certainly be a written story about his last days, his death and resurrection — the central story in the Gospel. In fact there would be several versions of that story. Not that any of these weren't true. It's just that each might recall some event and skip over another. So even when oral or spoken stories began to be turned into written stories we still don't have the New Testament. We have the next stage in the development of today's Gospels.

There's a lot we covered that is important, so let's review it here. An outline may help.

A Summary

1. The real basis of what the New Testament contains is what Jesus actually said and did.
2. While Jesus was alive doing and saying things, no one kept an accurate, day-to-day account.
3. The Apostles began to preach about Jesus only after they had experienced his resurrection and had become convinced that he was the Messiah. So when they preached it wasn't as reporters giving merely factual reports. Rather, they spoke out of faith and with the help of the Holy Spirit. They gave explanations, not just facts.
4. First they preached the story of Jesus' death and resurrection to prove to their Jewish audience that Jesus was, in fact, the promised Messiah they were waiting for.
5. The core message continued to grow in different situations:
   - New converts would ask questions and want to know more about Jesus.
   - New converts and the community began to face new problems and wanted to know what Jesus said about them.
   - The Apostles wanted to teach the community all that Jesus had taught them.
   - In special situations, like helping a sick member, the Apostles would tell stories about what Jesus did.
   - Especially at the eucharistic meal the community would share stories about Jesus' words and deeds.
   - Finally, collections of written stories, usually taking a particular theme (kingdom, parables, healing acts), were formed.

' gradually did it occur to people to write down the ies of Jesus.

So we can see that the New Testament we have today went through several stages of development. With that development, different versions of the same story came into being. We are now ready to take a look at how the New Testament in its present written form came about. We'll do that in the next chapter.

What Has This Got to Do With Me?

If you could talk to an Apostle today, what question would you ask him about Jesus? Why?

The Gospel stories only make sense to people who believe that Jesus is Messiah and Lord. Do they make sense to you?

The Scripture readings, or liturgy of the Word, at Mass are intended to tell us about Jesus. Do you pay enough attention?

DID YOU KNOW?

Jesus Spoke Aramaic

The language spoken by Jesus and the Apostles — and throughout Israel — was Aramaic. This language was the official language of the Persian Empire. When the Persians conquered the Jews, Aramaic replaced Hebrew as the daily Jewish language. In fact Aramaic was spoken throughout the Mideast until A.D. 635 when Syria fell to the Moslems. Today there is only one place in the world where you can find the "language of Jesus" spoken the way he spoke it. It is a little village named Ma'lula in a remote mountain region of Syria. Mark's Gospel preserved several Aramaic phrases such as *Talitha, koum,* which means, "Little girl, get up" (Mark 5.41), and *Ephphatha* meaning, "Be opened!" (Mark 7.34).

Review Questions and Activities

1. What is the first stage in the development of the New Testament?
2. What was the core message of the Apostles' preaching?
3. In what kinds of situations did the oral tradition grow?
4. What affected all of the Apostles' preaching?
5. How did today's Mass "begin"?

Scripture Focus

- *Acts 5.42*

The New Testament Is Written: A Faith History

Many have undertaken to compile a narrative of the events which have been fulfilled in our midst, precisely as those events were transmitted to us by the original eyewitnesses and ministers of the word.

(Luke 1.1-2)

We saw in the last chapter that the Apostles told the stories about Jesus' life. We also saw how the Apostles would apply these stories to meet the needs of their audience. This doesn't mean there were big differences, but there were differences. For example, in one story the teller might mention the exact place or exact time the event took place. Another might simply say, "Then one day," or "At another time," to introduce the same story. One teller might include details that another might leave out. Even the "sayings of Jesus" weren't always exactly the same since no one took down the exact words of Jesus when he spoke. But the key ideas, or sense, behind Jesus' words remained the same in the different versions. Also, sometimes the teller might add an explanation to what Jesus said. This explanation became connected with the words of Jesus himself. So at a later time, when the same story might be told, it would sound like the explanation was also part of what Jesus first said.

It Took Time

Now this doesn't mean the Apostles made up stories that didn't happen or that they deliberately made it sound like Jesus said things he didn't say. They believed Jesus was the Messiah so they were only trying to teach the people what Jesus had taught them. Also, as Jesus had promised, the Holy Spirit guided them when they preached. He helped them remember what they had forgotten. He helped them understand what had once confused them. Some of these stories were eventually written down, usually in the form of collections about some topic — miracles, parables, the kingdom, and the like. These earliest writings, however, didn't attempt to tell a "beginning-to-end" story about Jesus. Mostly they were read at the eucharistic meal when an Apostle wasn't present to tell them firsthand.

First Editions

This kind of oral teaching went on for about forty years after Jesus' death. Then various followers of Jesus attempted to write "beginning-to-end" stories about Jesus. They faced two tasks once they started. First, they had to decide what versions of a story they should use when several versions were available.

Second, they had to put some order into the events. There was some general order there. For example, Jesus' public life began after his baptism by John. It ended with his crucifixion three years later in Jerusalem. Much of the time in his early ministry took place in Galilee, and certain miracles took place there. He made several trips to Jerusalem, and certain events took place there. But it wasn't always clear where Jesus told some of his parables or just when he told them. It wasn't clear just where or when he performed some of his miracles.

This gave the authors some freedom when they came to organize the whole story. They could choose one version over another. They could have some events take place wherever they best fit into the story when it wasn't clear from the sources just when or where it did happen.

Who Did the Editing?

What did the authors use as a guide in making these kinds of choices? Several things. Often the version of a story they chose depended on the audience for whom they were writing. Also, each author would fit certain events and sayings into places where they would make the best sense in their overall version of the story. For example, Matthew tells the story of the Sermon on the Mount as a long speech by Jesus containing most of his key teachings. Chances are, many of the teachings were first given somewhere else or maybe later in Jesus' life. Jesus most likely said many of these things at various times to various groups as he preached throughout the country. Matthew chose to put them all together as one long speech because it fit into his approach to telling the overall story.

Finally, what most guided the authors of the Gospels was the Holy Spirit. He didn't sit on their shoulders and dictate to them. But he did stir up their hearts and their memories and imaginations as they recorded the words and actions of Jesus. In that sense the Holy Spirit is the real author of all Scripture. And the Gospels are a faithful rendering of the Word of God.

Then There Were Four

We said earlier that various followers attempted to tell the whole story in a written form. Some of the earliest attempts were popular for a while in one place or another but eventually were put aside as a better, more complete version was written. Often, though, as each version was written, authors would borrow ideas and even whole sections from the earlier version. Of all these only four survive. They are the four Gospels we have today. The community, with the help of the Holy Spirit, decided these four best told the "whole story" most accurately — each with a slightly different point of view. (To really come to know Jesus through the Scriptures we need all four Gospels.)

Have you thought of the Gospels as a special gift from God?

Mark Is First

Of the four Gospels — Matthew, Mark, Luke, and John — Mark's Gospel is the oldest. The author, borrowing from earlier sources, the oral tradition, and a living eyewitness (probably Peter, himself), wrote his version around A.D. 70. It's the shortest of the four, the most direct, and the simplest. Most experts agree that Mark's Gospel was written for non-Jewish converts at Rome — where Peter preached — to strengthen their faith and courage after the great persecutions began there.

Luke

Luke's Gospel was most probably written around A.D. 80. He introduces it this way:

> *Many have undertaken to compile a narrative of the events which have been fulfilled in our midst, precisely as those events were transmitted to us by the original eyewitnesses and ministers of the word. I too have carefully traced the whole sequence of events from the beginning and have decided to set it in writing for you, Theophilus. . . .*
>
> *(Luke 1.1-3)*

It's pretty clear from what Luke said that there had been other versions of the Gospel before him. He's also clear about why he's writing. Besides his friend Theophilus, he was writing for Gentile converts, probably around Asia Minor.

Luke was certainly aware of Mark's Gospel. He followed Mark's general outline, and even took whole sections word for word. But because he wrote for non-Jews, he skipped over details only Jews would appreciate and gave explanations of important Jewish customs his readers wouldn't have understood (for example, Sabbath laws, ritual washings). Most agree he traveled with Paul, wrote the Acts of the Apostles, and was the best Gospel writer when it came to grammar and writing style. He did his homework, as he said in the introduction, and was able to find out facts about Jesus' conception and birth that the other writers didn't mention.

Matthew

Matthew's Gospel was written about A.D. 85. He knew Mark's Gospel too and used it as a guide just as Luke did. But he was writing for Jewish converts to Christianity who lived in Syria. It seems one of his purposes was to encourage this community to hold fast to their faith that Jesus was the Messiah promised in the Old Testament. Their non-Christian, Jewish friends and relatives often persecuted them or tried to convince them in other ways that Jesus wasn't the Messiah. That's why Matthew uses a lot of Old Testament quotes about the Messiah and really gives the Jewish leaders of Jesus' time a bad name. They were the ones who rejected Jesus and should have known better.

Synoptic?

Mark's Gospel together with Luke's and Matthew's are often called the Synoptic Gospels. If you lined them up, passage by passage across a page, you could immediately see the similarities. (*Syn - optic* is Greek for looking at together.)

Then There Was John

With John's Gospel it is different. It

came much later, maybe even as late as A.D. 100.

By then a lot had happened in terms of the growth of the community of Jesus' followers we now call the Church. By then most local communities were familiar with and using one or more of the Synoptic Gospels. Persecutions had been numerous; Jerusalem and the Temple were destroyed. The people who had lived in Israel were driven throughout the world, both Jews and Christians.

The Apostles had traveled throughout the known world and preached Jesus. Only John was still alive. The rest had been martyred. So when John told his version of the Gospel (it's possible one of his disciples actually wrote it, but it is his version) he didn't bother repeating all that the other three Gospels had said. He took it for granted that his readers would know all

The Gospel took root in believers, and the Word spread.

about that. He gave a more behind-the-scenes account in one sense. He added stories overlooked by the others. He gave details they didn't cover. Just compare his Last Supper, crucifixion, and resurrection accounts with the other three Gospels.

Most important, he included within his Gospel over seventy years of growing understanding and faith about who Jesus is and what he means to all of us. In this sense, John's Gospel is a "theology" of Jesus, as well as an eyewitness history.

There you have it. Four final versions of the same life, words, and deeds of Jesus. They all have this in common:
• They were written *by* believers *for* believers.
• They are all based on eyewitness accounts of what Jesus said and did.
• They were all written in Greek, the best known written language of the time.
• They were all accepted by the believing community as the best, most accurate, most helpful versions of the story of Jesus that had been written.

Here are some differences:
• They were written at different times, for different groups, and for different purposes.
• They differ in overall length, style, in time sequence of certain events, and in the details of certain events.

What's the big deal? Just this. The more you come to know the Gospel messages and how they came to be, the better you'll be able to see them the way you should: as tools for meeting Jesus, your Messiah and your God, your Savior and your best friend.

What Has This Got to Do With Me?

Did you ever think that the Gospels were a special gift from God, our Father?
Why or why not?

Does it still bother you, or did it ever bother you, that the Gospels seem to differ so much?

What difference would it make to you if you could find a "scientific history/biography of Jesus" instead of the various faith-histories the Gospels contain?

DID YOU KNOW?

Beyond the Gospels

The New Testament contains twenty-seven "books." Four are the Gospels. One is called the Acts of the Apostles, which is an account of the adventure of the Apostles and the early Church from the ascension of Jesus to Paul's imprisonment in Rome. Another is a kind of mystical-poetic-mystery book about the future. It's called the Book of Revelation. Then there are twenty-one letters or epistles (Greek for letter), written by various Apostles to various communities of believers from about A.D. 50-100. Paul wrote most of these letters but the other authors are Peter, John, James, and Jude. Since most of these letters tried to help people deal with the definite problems they faced as followers of Jesus, they were read at the eucharistic meal along with readings from the Gospels. So they got attached to the Gospels as means of teaching about Jesus and telling his story.

The letters, Acts, and Revelation didn't develop like the Gospels. They were "one shot" writings for a definite purpose. That's why we don't have all kinds of versions of these "books."

All these books — Gospels, letters, Acts of the Apostles, and Revelation taken together — are what we call the New Testament.

Here's a list of the books and when they were probably written:

1 Thessalonians	49-51
2 Thessalonians	49-51
Galatians	50-54
1 Corinthians	56
2 Corinthians	57
Romans	57
Mark	60-70
James	60 (95)
Ephesians	61-63
Philippians	62-63
Colossians	62-63
Philemon	62-63
1 Timothy	63-67 (90)
2 Timothy	63-67 (90)
Titus	63-67 (90)
1 Peter	64
Luke	70-80
Matthew	85 (80-100)
Hebrews	80-90
Acts	70-90
John	90-100
1 John	90-100
2 John	90-100
3 John	90-100
Jude	90-100
Revelation	94-95
2 Peter	102

Review Questions and Activities

1. About when did written Gospels begin?
2. How many Gospels survived and what are their names?
3. What choices did the authors of the Gospels have to make?
4. What kept the authors of the New Testament, especially the Gospels, from making up their own stories?

Scripture Focus

- *Luke 1.1-2*

Unit Review

1. What does the name Jesus mean?
2. What is the difference between being resurrected and being brought back to life?
3. When did messianism begin? What is it?
4. Describe each of the major religious groups in Jesus' time.
5. Describe how oral tradition grew and why it grew.
6. What kept the authors of the Gospels from making up their own stories?

Some Words to Know

CHRIST • The Greek word for anointed one or Messiah.

CONVERTS • Those who have changed from one religion to another.

COVENANT • An agreement, either between persons or between God and a person or people.

CRUCIFIXION • The manner of putting someone to death by means of nailing or binding the victim on a cross.

ESSENES • A religious group who lived much as our monks do today, in communities apart from the rest of people.

EUCHARISTIC MEAL • The celebration of the people of God during which the Body and Blood of Jesus is shared.

GALILEE • The northernmost area of Palestine, home of Jesus.

JERUSALEM • The capital of Palestine and center of all Jewish life.

JESUS • Hebrew name meaning "Yahweh saves."

JEW • One who is a member of the Hebrew people and belongs to the religion which follows the Law of Moses.

JORDAN RIVER • The largest river of Palestine, which flows from Mt. Hermon in the north through the Sea of

Galilee to the Dead Sea in the south.

JUDEA • The southern section of Palestine with Jerusalem for its capital.

LEPER • Any person with a skin disease (at the time of Jesus).

MESSIAH • Hebrew word meaning "the anointed one"; it came to be applied to the person who would be sent by Yahweh to save his people.

MESSIANISM • The beliefs held by those expecting a Messiah.

NAZARETH • Small town in Galilee where Jesus grew up.

ORAL TRADITION • The handing down from generation to generation by word of mouth any information, especially doctrines and teachings.

PASSOVER • The special supper celebrated each year by the Jews to commemorate their passage from Egypt to the promised land.

PHARISEES • (Means separated ones); those who adhered to a strict following of the Law.

PILGRIMAGE • A journey to a shrine for a religious purpose; that is, for worship, to fulfill a promise, or to seek spiritual aid.

PRIESTS • A member of the priestly family with certain privileges.

PROPHET • A person who proclaims a message from God.

PUBLICANS • Tax collectors who worked for the Romans.

RABBI • A teacher. One who led the services in the synagogue and answered questions the people would ask.

RELIGION • A body of beliefs and manner of worshiping God.

RESURRECTION • The physical rising from death by Jesus Christ. The rising again to life of all the human dead before the final judgment.

SADDUCEES • (From Sadoc, a priest at the time of David); members of the priestly family.

SAMARITANS • A mixed people descending from the Israelites who lived near the city of Sichem. They were rivals of the Israelites and were looked down upon by them.

SCRIBES • Learned men of the Law.

SPIRITUAL • Refers to supernatural, ecclesiastical, religious, or sacred matters, especially those aspects of life that are beyond the physical.

SYNOPTIC • The Greek word for "looking at together." The term that came to be applied to the Gospels of Matthew, Mark, and Luke.

TEMPLE • An enclosed place of worship; for the Jews, the sacred building in Jerusalem which was the center of all their faith and religion.

ZEALOTS • A political group who sought to drive the Romans out of Israel by force.

UNIT 2

Ministry, Message, and Miracles

INTRODUCTION

In this unit we will see how Jesus was called to his ministry and how he prepared himself for it. Then we'll see how he actually went about his ministry — the special qualities he had, which prompted people to call him the greatest teacher who ever lived.

Actually his message was rather simple. He taught about his Father and about his Father's kingdom to which we are all called. But his teaching was also revolutionary. It touched people's hearts, not just their minds. It changed people's lives, not just their ideas. The world has never been the same since the carpenter's son from Nazareth began wandering the Galilean countryside talking to those who would listen.

Jesus was known as a miracle worker as well as a teacher. But we'll see that Jesus' miracles were actually a central part of his teaching. They were signs, demonstrations that the kingdom he proclaimed and taught was actually at hand. They were proofs that Jesus was really God's messenger and that the people should listen to him. They were never performed to amuse or awe the crowd.

As you read this unit, try to imagine yourself as one of the people in the crowd, hearing and watching Jesus as he taught and performed miracles. How do you think you might have felt?

Jesus and John the Baptizer

Here begins the gospel of Jesus Christ, the Son of God. In Isaiah the prophet it is written:

"I send my messenger before you
to prepare your way:
a herald's voice in the desert,
crying,
'Make ready the way of the
Lord,
clear him a straight path.' "

Thus it was that John the Baptizer appeared in the desert, proclaiming a baptism of repentance which led to forgiveness of sins. All the Judean countryside and the people of Jerusalem went out to him in great numbers. They were being baptized by him in the Jordan River as they confessed their sins. John was clothed in camel's hair, and wore a leather belt around his waist. His food was grasshoppers and wild honey. The theme of his preaching was: "One more powerful than I is to come after me. I am not fit to stoop and untie his sandal straps. I have baptized you in water; he will baptize you in the Holy Spirit."

During that time, Jesus came from Nazareth in Galilee and was baptized in the Jordan by John. Immediately on coming out of the water he saw the sky rent in two and the Spirit descending on him like a dove. Then a voice came from the heavens: "You are my beloved Son. On you my favor rests."

(Mark 1.1-11)

End and Beginning

That's how Mark's Gospel begins. That's how Jesus' mission begins. And that's how John the Baptizer's mission ends. That's how the Old Testament ends and the New Testament begins.

John the Baptizer was clearly a prophet, the last and the greatest of the Old Testament prophets. His mission was to complete what all the other prophets had begun: to announce the immediate coming of the Messiah. Once he recognized that Jesus was the Messiah he pointed him out to his followers. He knew his mission was over. He was no longer needed. That's why he began to tell his followers: "He must increase, while I must decrease" (John 3.30).

We actually know very little about

John. Yet he played a major role in the history of salvation. So much so that Jesus even said about him, "There is no man born of woman greater than John" (Luke 7.28).

Some Facts

Here are a few things we do know. John's father, Zechariah, was a priest of the Jewish religion. His wife, Elizabeth, was a cousin of Mary, the mother of Jesus. This means John and Jesus were related, maybe as second cousins. Since John's mother was sterile before his conception, and since both parents were quite old, they took his birth as a special sign that Yahweh had a religious role for him.

You can read all about this in Luke, Chapter 1. You might want to read it now.

Did John and Jesus know each other when they were growing up? We know they were born within a few months of each other. We know that Mary was a special cousin to Elizabeth and that they had visited each other before the births. We know that Mary and Joseph lived in Nazareth when Jesus was growing up. We know that Elizabeth and Zechariah lived near Jerusalem, some distance away. But we also know that Mary and Joseph went to the major festivals in Jerusalem. So maybe at those times they would stay with or at least visit Elizabeth and Zechariah. There is a good chance that John and

Jesus met each other as small children. Maybe they even played games together.

A Prophet's Lifestyle

It's obvious that John was a very religious person. He was a prophet, after all. He lived a very disciplined life. That means he avoided a lot of the normal pleasures most people enjoy — like eating fancy foods and drinking wine, and wearing fancy clothes. He spent most of his time out of doors; he wore clothes made of camel's hair — the clothes of the very poor. He lived off the land eating things like locusts (there is a kind in desert regions that is okay to eat) and wild honey. He was hardly a "junk food" addict. He let his beard and hair grow.

Some say he belonged to or at least lived with the Essenes. We saw that this

The River Jordan where Jesus was baptized.

sect was very strict, followed the Covenant to the letter, fasted, prayed, and practiced ritual bathing. The Essenes had a kind of monastery in the desert east of Jerusalem, near the Jordan River. That's were John preached and baptized.

John must have looked a little scary with his camel-hair robe, long hair and beard, and thin wiry body from his diet. But he was certainly clean. He believed in ritual washing (baptism) as an outward sign of inner purity.

In his time there were a lot of phony prophets. Times were bad and people were hoping Yahweh would send a prophet. They'd listen to anyone with a hopeful message — at least for a while. But John was different and the people could tell it. He really lived what he preached. He talked with real belief.

That's why so many people came to hear him and to be baptized by him. They came from Jerusalem, not just the countryside. His followers included Roman soldiers, Pharisees, merchants, and tax collectors. They listened to him, believed him, turned from sin, and were baptized.

Then It Happened

Then Jesus came. John was startled. Somehow he knew this man, a few months younger than himself, was the *Messiah.* Did he expect it? Somehow he did know. His cousin, Jesus, was the Messiah! We can read about it in John 1.19-34.

As we said, John's mission ended with the baptism of Jesus. He did continue to preach and call people to repent. But as soon as Jesus began his own ministry John encouraged people to follow Jesus instead of himself. Then, not too long after Jesus began his preaching, John was arrested by Herod, the Jewish king. Herod was living in adultery with his brother's wife. John had publicly accused the king of this sin, since it was a scandal to the people.

Actually Herod had a lot of respect for John and knew that he was a holy man, maybe even a prophet as in the old days. He visited John in prison and talked with him. But his "wife" hated John because of the things John had said about her. Finally she found a way to trick Herod into having John killed. You can read about it in Mark 6.14-29.

A Lesson For Us?

John was beheaded. He died a martyr like so many of the other Old Testament prophets. But he had completed his special mission of proclaiming the arrival of the long-awaited Messiah. We don't know why God chose John for that special mission, any more than we know why God chose Mary as Jesus' mother. But we do know that John, like Mary, fulfilled his mission perfectly.

We can learn a lot from John as we try to follow God's special call for each of us. He was always humble even though great crowds followed him. Many even thought John might be the Messiah. He never lost sight of his task — to prepare the way, not get in the way. He was brave. He proclaimed the truth even though it meant risking his life. He was self-disciplined.

No wonder Jesus admired him and in many ways imitated him in carrying out his own mission. That wouldn't be a bad idea for us either.

What Has This Got to Do With Me?

Do you think God may have some special mission for you some day?

Are there some ways you need to become more self-disciplined?

Are you willing to take the risk of being laughed at in order to do and say what you know is right?

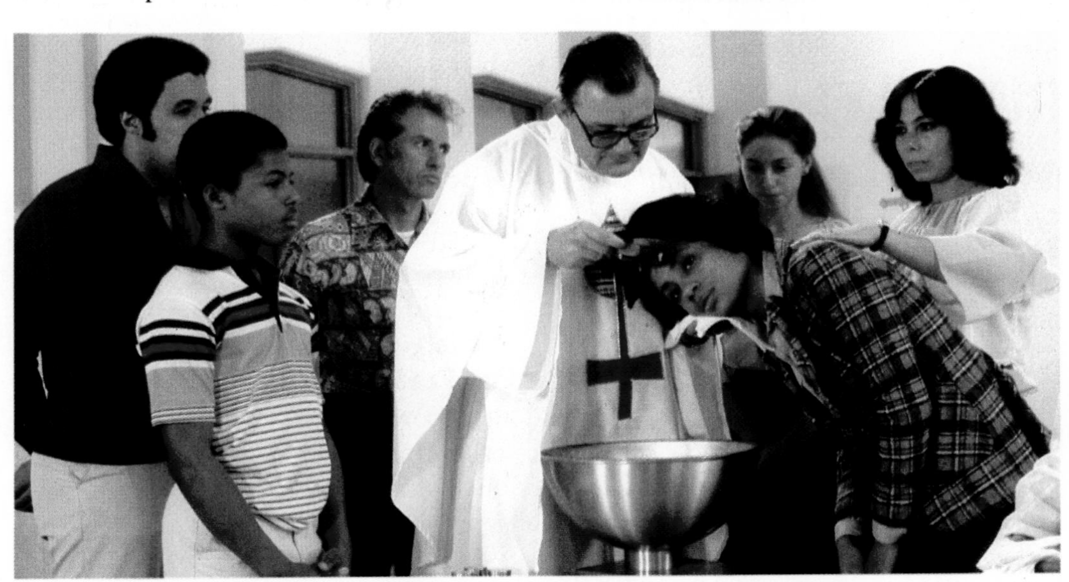

Through the sacrament of baptism, we join with the community of believers in becoming one with Jesus.

DID YOU KNOW?

Cleansed in Christ

Jesus never baptized, but his followers used baptism as the way to bring converts into the Church. Actually, baptism has been used by many religions, as a rite, or sign (ritual sign), of cleansing from sins. Hindus, for example, bathe in the Ganges River as a sign of ritual cleansing. Many of the pagan religions, called mystery religions, popular before and at the time of Jesus, used baptism as a way of introducing new members. It had much the same meaning as it has for the Church today — dying to a sinful life and being reborn as a "new" person.

In primitive tribes, even today, their nature religions require a baptism of the newborn child as a sign of cleansing away the impurities involved in birth. Often they use the occasion as a name-giving ceremony much as we do in the Church.

So, in some ways, this cleansing rite is not unique to the Church. Yet in one way it is entirely unique because it is a sacrament. Through it we receive the very life and Spirit of Jesus. Through it we become one with Jesus, with his dying and with his resurrection.

Review Questions and Activities

1. Why is John considered the greatest of the Old Testament prophets?
2. What are some of John's special qualities?
3. How and why did John die?
4. What was John's relationship with Jesus?
5. Describe the events surrounding the conception and birth of John.

Scripture Focus

- *Mark 1.2-3*

"I send my messenger before you
to prepare your way:
a herald's voice in the desert,
crying,
'Make ready the way of the
Lord,
clear him a straight path.' "

CHAPTER 8

Jesus in the Desert

At that point the Spirit sent him out toward the desert. He stayed in the wasteland forty days, put to the test there by Satan. He was with the wild beasts, and angels waited on him.

(Mark 1.12-13)

Why a Desert?

It's rather common for a person, facing a really tough decision, to go off alone for a while to have time to think and pray about it.

That's what Jesus did right after his baptism by John. That baptism was a special religious experience for Jesus. During it he knew that Yahweh was calling him for a special mission. The Gospel writers describe this experience in terms of a dove coming upon Jesus and Yahweh's voice coming from heaven, calling Jesus his son.

Jesus knew he had a special relationship with Yahweh. He knew he wanted to devote his life to serving the Father. He was about to begin his ministry in earnest. It was a powerful "moment" in his life. He had to think and pray about it. So he went into the desert.

Possibly the scene of Jesus' temptations.

What a Desert!

And what a desert! Southern Judea around the Dead Sea is not a desert like those in the movies — all sand with an oasis here and there. It was hilly, rocky, dry — more like the Dakota Badlands. Water was almost impossible to find. Almost nothing grew. It was full of snakes, scorpions, some larger wild animals.

How did Jesus survive there? We don't

know. One Gospel account says he fasted (Matthew 4.2), which means he drank only enough to stay alive. St. Luke tells us he "ate nothing" (Luke 4.2). He became extremely weak and hungry.

Temptation Is Real

In the desert Jesus had time to think and pray. He was alone. At least for a while. All the Gospel writers agree that Satan came and tempted him. Since he was alone at the time, he must have told his followers about the experience at some later time. Otherwise we wouldn't know what took place. Jesus told his followers about it because the temptations he experienced would be the kind they — and we — would have to face. You can read about the temptations in Matthew 4.1-11 and in Luke 4.1-13. Why don't you do it now?

Satan Is No Dummy

Satan is no dummy. He knows how we humans think and he knows all about our weak spots. He used that knowledge when he tempted Jesus. First he went after Jesus' physical needs. He suggested that Jesus turn stones into bread so he could satisfy his hunger. Jesus taught us an important lesson when he rejected that temptation. Our spiritual life is much more important than physical needs and physical pleasures. Sure, we must take care of our physical needs, but we should never make them so important that we neglect our spiritual life or our relationship with God. That can be very hard today when so much of society makes seeking physical pleasure the most important thing. Physical pleasure is the basic message in most advertising, in many TV programs and movies. And it's a temptation just like the one Jesus experienced in the desert.

"All these will I bestow on you if you prostrate yourself in homage before me."

The next temptation is trickier. Satan went after our human desire to be famous, popular, liked by everyone. Who doesn't want to hear praise?

Who wouldn't want people to recognize

them, seek them out, follow them around. But Jesus knew, and he teaches us, that popularity isn't worth much if it means betraying our friendship with God. There will be many times when we must choose between being popular, going along with the crowd, pleasing our friends, and being true to God. Often that choice is much tougher than deciding to give up some physical pleasure for God.

Finally Satan went after our most dangerous human weakness, pride and the desire for power. This might not be such a big temptation for you just now. But it is real for you even now. Who wouldn't want to get their own way, control others, be able to make all the decisions for the group. Who wouldn't prefer to make their own rules rather than have to follow the rules others make? Who doesn't want to be his own boss?

That's why some people end up worshiping power rather than God. They make power their God. Jesus teaches us this is perhaps the biggest mistake we can make — and the worst temptation of all.

What We Can Learn

Each of these was a real temptation for Jesus, and he would have to face them many times in his ministry. The letter to the Hebrews (4.15) says he "was tempted in every way that we are, yet never sinned." Jesus understands what it's like when we experience temptations. In any event, Satan could see he wasn't getting anywhere with Jesus and left him — for a while. Something happened to Jesus during those forty days in the desert. He "returned in the power of the Spirit" (Luke 4.14). It was maybe a final preparation for his mission.

Jesus knew the Hebrew Scriptures very well. He was familiar with all the prophecies about the Messiah — how he would be rejected and eventually killed. Jesus' decision to answer God's call wasn't an easy one. Also Satan's suggestions to start off by doing wonders, like floating down from the Temple to gain recognition, must have had real appeal. But he rejected those temptations, choosing to follow only God's will for him. And that's how Jesus acted throughout his ministry. He never looked back; he never tried to take the easy way out, although he was tempted to. He always obeyed the Father, even though that ultimately meant death on the cross.

When Jesus came out of the desert, he didn't know exactly what would happen next or just what God would ask him to do. What he did know was this: he must proclaim the kingdom of God. He remained open to the Spirit's direction. There would be other times that Jesus would return to the desert or at least go off by himself to pray. He would need to seek his Father's will when he faced key decisions like selecting his Apostles.

What temptations do we feel in our lives today?

But once Jesus came out of the desert after his forty-day fast, his public ministry began. It would not end until three years later in Jerusalem, hanging on a cross.

But as we know, his death was not actually the end of his ministry. In a real sense that was the beginning.

Go to the Desert

Jesus' desert experience not only taught us the kinds of temptations we can expect in our own lives. It also teaches us that there will be times in our own lives when we will need to "go to the desert" to pray, to come closer to God, to seek his guidance in making decisions and seeking his will for us.

More than ever today we need to find "desert places" where we can get away from all the noise and distractions offered by radio, TV and such.

What Has This Got to Do With Me?

What are some of my biggest temptations? How do I deal with them?

Do I need a desert place? Where is my desert place?

How often do I seek God's help and guidance in making important decisions?

DID YOU KNOW?

The Desert Fathers

A few centuries after Jesus' death and resurrection many of his Christian followers imitated him by leaving the busy cities to live in desert places. They would find a cave or build a little hut. They would live off the land or maybe raise a little garden. But most of the time they fasted or ate very little in imitation of Jesus. They spent much of their time in prayer. Though they went out to be alone, many soon gained a reputation for holiness. People from the cities would come and seek them out. They would ask these holy men to pray for them and to teach them about God. Some even stayed right there in the desert and began to live near the holy men and imitate their way of life. Gradually whole communities of desert-dwelling holy people developed. It was from such communities that religious or monastic life gradually came about. In many ways, monasteries are like desert places. They are free of the distractions of the world. The men and women who live there spend much of their time in prayer and fasting like Jesus.

Yet, it is from just such monasteries that some of our greatest saints and Church leaders have come — popes, theologians, saints of all kinds. Who said nothing can grow in a desert? Obviously, holiness can grow in a desert!

Review Questions and Activities

1. Why did Jesus go into the desert?
2. Describe the three temptations as told to us by the Gospel writers.
3. What form do those temptations take for us?
4. What forms can those temptations take for a seventh grader?
5. Why do we need a desert place?

Scripture Focus

- *Mark 1.12-13*

CHAPTER 9

Jesus the Teacher

All who were present spoke favorably of him; they marveled at the appealing discourse which came from his lips. They also asked, "Is not this Joseph's son?"

(Luke 4.22)

Jesus was given many titles in the New Testament but the one most used, and the one he seemed to prefer the most, was Teacher. In Hebrew it is rabboni or rabbi. Basically that's what Jesus' public ministry involved: teaching the people about the Father and about the Father's kingdom. When he wasn't teaching the crowds he was teaching his Apostles so they would be able to continue after him.

Who's a Teacher?

But Jesus wasn't a teacher as we think of teachers today — standing in a classroom with a textbook. And he didn't teach like most of the other rabbis of his time. Most rabbis in Jesus' time would simply recite Scripture passages and give prepared explanations about how people should act. This kind of teaching tended to be dry, boring. Since few people could read, the teachers often tended to be proud and look down on them. Also the teachers in Jesus' time usually had a fixed place where they taught, like a synagogue. People had to come to them.

Obviously, Jesus wasn't proud. He didn't look down on the people. He certainly didn't just recite Scripture passages or give pat answers. His teaching was fresh, exciting, surprising. As the people themselves commented, he taught with authority, not like the scribes and Pharisees (Mark 2.5-12). That means he taught with conviction, enthusiasm, and real concern for the people and for his message.

Jesus did teach in synagogues many times on the Sabbath day. But he was a wandering teacher. He went where the people were. Any time a group would gather he would take the opportunity to teach them. He sought out the people. He just didn't wait for them to come to him. Because of that people came to him any time they heard he was in the area.

Jesus came out of the desert to proclaim the kingdom, and people began to listen. But Jesus wasn't a good

Any time a group gathered, Jesus took time to teach them.

teacher just because he had a fresh message or just because he went out to the people. There was more to it.

He Knew His Audience

He was good because he used familiar, everyday things to explain the great truths of life. While his audience usually included people from all walks of life, mostly they were common people. Jesus grew up with the common people. He understood their problems and concerns, how they lived and how they worked, the day-to-day situations they faced. In most of his stories, he used these familiar things so people could understand.

Here is a list of such stories for you to look up and read. They give an idea of what we mean:

- The Sower (Luke 8.4-15).
- The Lost Coin and The Lost Sheep (Luke 15.3-10).
- The Rich Man and Lazarus (Luke 16.19-31).
- The Good Samaritan (Luke 10.25-37).
- The Prodigal Son (Luke 15.11-32).

- Parable of the Tenant Farmers (Luke 20.9-19).
- The Mustard Seed (Mark 4.30-34).
- The Merciless Official (Matthew 18.21-35).

All of these stories have their roots in the everyday life, customs, and practices of his time. In other words, Jesus really knew his audience and understood them.

Parables Are Best

Stories, or parables, were one of Jesus' favorite ways to teach. Parable means "a comparison." Jesus would compare something familiar like shepherding or planting or fishing to the higher truth he was sharing. Because they are stories with some drama in them, they hold our attention. They are also easy to remember and retell. Usually the truth they teach is easy to see, so there is no need for explanation. Sometimes, however, Jesus would have to help the people understand it. Sometimes Jesus would make shorter comparisons or similes. These are like parables but they don't really have a story with them. An example would be Matthew 13.44.

But Jesus didn't just teach with stories. He would often simply comment on something that was happening and help his followers see the lesson it contained. Good examples of this are the widow's A good example of this is the widow's mite (Luke 21.1-5); the question of the Sabbath (Luke 6.1-11); the ambition of James and John (Mark 10.35-45); and the example of the rich young man (Mark 10.17-31).

Then there were times when Jesus taught in a more formal and direct sense. The Sermon on the Mount (Matthew 5-6) contains a collection of the best examples of this kind of teaching.

Actions Speak Too

Jesus also taught by his actions, his example. He taught patience, humility, gentleness, and forgiveness by being patient, humble, gentle, and forgiving. The Apostles weren't likely to forget, for instance, when Jesus drove the

Jesus taught patience, humility, gentleness, and forgiveness by being patient, gentle, and forgiving.

money changers out of the Temple (John 2.13-17); how he dealt with the Samaritan woman at the well (John 4.4-42); how he treated the little children (Luke 18.15-17); and how he dealt with the woman taken in adultery (John 8.1-11). Most of all, they would remember how he washed their feet at the Last Supper and how he acted throughout his Passion. That's why the Gospels are filled with stories of what Jesus did, as well as what he said. We can learn what it means to be Christian from everything Jesus did.

Jesus' miracles are lessons too. They were more than signs of the power the Father had given him. Behind most of the miracles we can see what moved Jesus — concern for the sick, the outcasts, the poor, and the suffering. It was this concern that moved him to help the widow of Naim (Luke 7.11-17), the deaf-mute (Mark 7.31-37), and the man with the withered hand (Mark 3.1-6). It was his concern for the people that moved him to multiply the loaves and fishes (Luke 9.10-17).

An Ongoing Problem

Jesus faced one problem, though, as he went around teaching, giving example, and performing miracles. Many of the

Jewish leaders felt he was teaching false doctrine because he didn't follow their "official" interpretation of the Law. They were also afraid because he was gaining such a large following. They seemed, quite frankly, jealous of his success and popularity. And many times Jesus openly challenged their teachings and showed the people errors in them. It seems that these leaders would follow Jesus everywhere he went. They kept hoping to catch him in some obviously false doctrine. They kept trying to find ways to make him look foolish and to turn the people from him. A few of the best-known examples of this were when they tried to trick him regarding paying taxes to Caesar and when they brought the adulteress to him. Read Mark 12.13-17 and John 8.1-11.

As these two stories show, Jesus always ended up turning the tables on them. The people loved it!

There is one other thing we should see about Jesus, the Teacher. Like any good teacher, he hated false teaching as much as he loved truth. He could become really angry at times when he felt the people were being misled by the teachings of the Jewish leaders.

One example of when he really "blew up" at them can be found in Matthew 15.1-14. You can almost feel the anger in his words.

Summary

Jesus taught with stories, or parables, and other comparisons. He taught by explaining the meaning behind an event. Sometimes he taught in a more formal way, giving a longer talk about some truth or virtue. All his actions were lessons for us. This includes his miracles. Even if we aren't able to do the miracles, we are expected to imitate Jesus' love and concern for those who need help.

There's no doubt Jesus is Teacher. What other teacher in the world could ever say things like this and mean it? "Learn from me for I am meek and humble of heart," and "I am the Way, the Truth and the Life."

Next we'll begin taking a look at what Jesus, the teacher, taught.

What Has This Got to Do With Me?

Am I taking the opportunity to learn from Jesus?

Have I really learned what it means to be a Christian?

What do I most need to learn from Jesus right now?

DID YOU KNOW?

Socrates the Teacher

Jesus is generally recognized as the greatest teacher in history, even by those who don't believe he is the Son of God. The only one who comes close to him is a man named Socrates. He lived in Greece during its Golden Age, several hundred years before Jesus.

He was similar to Jesus in many ways. He loved truth. He was humble. He gathered disciples (students) around him and taught them informally, as much by what he did as by what he said.

The leaders of his day hated him, felt he was leading the youth astray, were jealous of his popularity. Eventually they killed him.

His followers, like Jesus' followers, kept his teachings alive, though. One of his most famous disciples, Plato, wrote a series of stories called *Dialogues* which was a kind of gospel for Socrates' followers.

Even today people study these *Dialogues* and learn from them. Another famous follower of Socrates was Aristotle. His writings eventually had a great influence on Christians as they tried to explain Jesus' teachings to the pagan world.

Review Questions and Activities

1. What is a parable?
2. Why was Jesus so popular as a teacher?
3. Why didn't the Jewish leaders like Jesus?
4. What can we learn from the miracles of Jesus?
5. Give an example of each of the following forms of Jesus' teaching method: parable or story, use of an event taking place, example, formal talk.

Scripture Focus

- *Luke 4.22*

Jesus' Message: God's Reign Is Here

After John's arrest Jesus appeared in Galilee proclaiming the good news of God: "This is the time of fulfillment. The reign of God is at hand! Reform your lives and believe in the gospel!"

(Mark 1.14-15)

That simple announcement by Jesus is the core of his message: the reign of God is here. For centuries, ever since the rule of David, the Jewish people had been looking for and hoping for God to establish a perfect kingdom. Its king would be the promised Messiah.

Old Testament prophets often described what that reign would be like. It would be a kingdom where justice and peace are the order of the day. The poor would no longer be oppressed by the rich. The weak would no longer be abused by the powerful. God himself would be their protector, and his Messiah would carry out all God's commands.

Over the centuries, as we've seen, the people began to think in terms of an earthly kingdom and a warrior Messiah who would lead them to victory over their conquerors. But they did not totally lose sight of the kind of kingdom of peace and justice the prophets talked about.

Good News

Jesus came, then, announcing the Good News, the Gospel. The long-awaited reign of God has arrived!

All of Jesus' other teaching and working with the people is basically his attempt to convince them of this Good News, to show them the true nature of God's kingdom, and to call them to accept God's rule by reforming their lives. That's what his whole public life was all about.

Repent

What did Jesus teach us about this reign of God? One of the first things is the need for repentance, for a change of life, for reform. That's how a person enters into the kingdom — by giving up old practices of injustice, cruelty, selfishness, sensuality, hatred, and fighting. Jesus called people to surrender their lives to God, to let God, rather than the powers of evil, rule over them. God's reign is not forced on us. We must freely accept it. That's what Jesus asked of people. That's what he expected of anyone who would be his disciple.

Mercy Is the Name of the Game

But Jesus did more than call people to repentance. He gave them hope. Jesus taught that one of the central things about God's reign is God's mercy. No matter how bad a person had been, forgiveness was always possible. There was no sin so great that God's mercy couldn't overcome it. Many of Jesus' parables deal with the mercy of God. Probably the most famous is the one about the prodigal son. Many of Jesus' own actions showed us God's mercy too. Jesus went especially to people regarded as public sinners: tax collectors, prostitutes, Samaritans. Many of these became his special friends. Why? Because they became convinced that God would forgive them. They were often the first to repent and change their lives. Look at Mary Magdalene, Zacchaeus the tax collector, the Samaritan woman, the woman taken in adultery. What Jesus

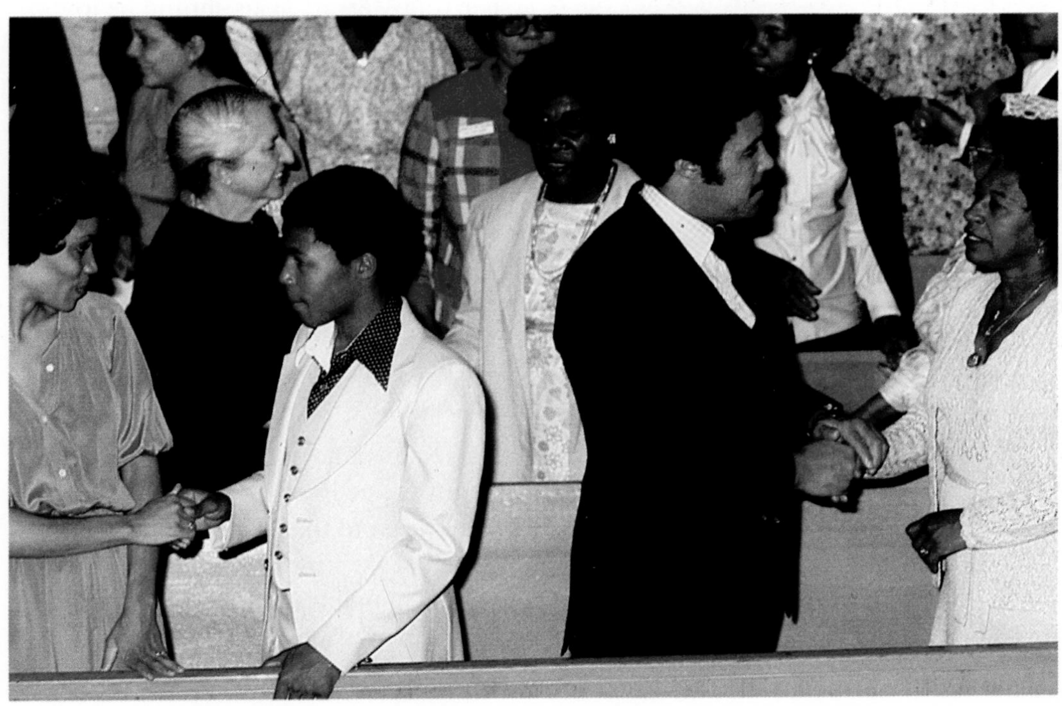

Jesus taught that one of the central things about God's reign is God's mercy.

really taught was that no one would be kept out of the kingdom because of past sins. Whoever seeks forgiveness will receive it.

Salvation Too

What can people expect to find in the kingdom? Jesus taught that we will find salvation! Salvation first of all means freedom from the powers of evil, freedom from slavery to sin. But with that freedom comes wholeness, protection from harm, freedom from the effects of sin such as sickness and death. That's the real meaning behind most of Jesus' miracles and exorcisms (exorcism = drive out the evil spirit). Jesus showed the people that the kingdom had really arrived by showing his power over the forces of evil. Evil spirits were no match for him. All he needed to do was give a simple command and they would flee. People who believed saw this as real proof that God's reign had begun. But many of the Jewish leaders refused to believe. They even accused Jesus of working with the devil, not against him. That made Jesus very angry (read Mark 3.20-30).

Many of Jesus' cures showed the same kind of salvation that the kingdom promises. That the blind would see, the deaf hear, and the lame walk were some of the signs, according to the prophets, that God's reign had arrived. So Jesus' cures showed the kind of salvation or wholeness we can expect to find in God's kingdom.

We Will Overcome

Another important thing Jesus taught about the kingdom was that it would succeed, no matter how hard people tried to prevent it. Many of his kingdom parables make that point. One of the best examples is that of the sower (Luke 8.4-15). Jesus also taught that, though the reign of God may begin slowly, it would continue to grow and grow. That's what the parable of the mustard seed teaches.

Rejoice, Alleluia

Finally Jesus taught us that the reign of God should be a source of great joy. The followers of Jesus should be joyful, not sad. They should be filled with hope and peace, not worries and fears. Jesus often compared the kingdom to a banquet or feast. What can be a more joyful thing than a banquet, surrounded by friends, music, good food and drink? To enter into the kingdom does mean giving up a former way of living. But it also means going to a feast or party. To enter the kingdom is a cause for joy, not sorrow.

Those are some of the key things Jesus taught the people about the kingdom. Keep in mind that announcing the arrival of the kingdom and explaining it was his main message. It would also be the main message of his disciples after him.

The final proof Jesus offered that the

The reign of God may begin slowly, but it will grow and grow if our hearts remain open.

reign of God had indeed come was his own resurrection. Death itself is conquered when God establishes his reign. In God's kingdom there will be no lasting death. That's what Jesus' resurrection teaches.

Nonbelievers

Jesus proclaimed the arrival of the kingdom. This doesn't mean everyone believed him. In fact many people were angered by his teaching. A good example is in Luke 4.16-30. It may be hard for us, nearly two thousand years later, to understand how people could be so blind. But we must remember a few things. As we pointed out in the first chapter, Jesus didn't have very good credentials, by society's standards. He came from a poorer class, had no formal education, and no official position. People were looking for a different kind of Messiah at the time.

Also there had been many false prophets around Jesus' time (Jesus warned his own followers there would be more after him). These false prophets would get the people stirred up and excited. Then nothing would happen, and the people would be disappointed. So people were on their guard. Just because some carpenter from Nazareth said God's reign had begun wasn't enough for them. They'd need more proof.

But what about the miracles? That is a tough one. It would seem Jesus' miracles would be all the proof people needed. We must remember, though, that many of Jesus' miracles were

Not this kind of kingdom!

performed in private, or with just a few people around. News of them would have to come secondhand to many people. Imagine today if someone came to you and said he just saw some holy person cure a blind man. You'd probably have your doubts.

Some of Jesus' miracles, of course, like the multiplication of the loaves and fishes, took place in front of thousands of people. The problem there was that they missed the point of the miracle. Jesus did it out of concern for the hungry people, and to show that sharing was a key ingredient in God's kingdom. But the people wanted to make him king, not of God's kingdom, but of an earthly kingdom. How great it would be to have a king who could produce bread like that! No one in his kingdom would ever have to work again. Think how easy it would be to supply armies with Jesus as king. That's why Jesus went and hid himself after that miracle. They wanted him as king of the kingdom, but for the wrong reasons, and of the wrong kingdom.

Don't Forget Selfishness

There's one final reason to explain why people didn't accept Jesus and his message. Maybe it's the most important. Some people just don't want to change. They don't want to give up their lifestyle. They don't want to give up their pet ideas, the power they have over others, their position in society. They don't want to have to forgive their enemies or to treat the poor and weak as their equals. In other words, Jesus' message of repentance and reform was too hard for many — especially those who had the most to lose — like the religious leaders and wealthy people. Maybe that's why most of Jesus' followers came from the poor, the weak, the sinners and outcasts. They had the most to gain and the least to lose by believing that the kingdom of God had arrived. They were open-minded.

For whatever reason, we know many people refused to accept Jesus or only accepted him for a while. (Remember the parable of the sower?) But isn't that true today also? The key thing to remember in all of this, though, is that the core message of Jesus was the arrival of God's reign. Everything he said and did can be better understood in that light. Next, we'll take a look at what Jesus said about the God whose kingdom he was proclaiming.

What Has This Got to Do With Me?

What changes would you have to make in your own lifestyle in order to let God rule over you?

What would salvation mean for you right now?

Are you joyful because you are a Christian or despite it?

Review Questions and Activities

1. What were some of the key things about the reign of God that Old Testament prophets told us?
2. What was Jesus' core message throughout his ministry?
3. What is the one condition for gaining admission into the kingdom, according to Jesus?
4. Why is Jesus' teaching about God's mercy so important to the kingdom?
5. What role did Jesus' miracles and exorcisms play in his teaching about the kingdom?

Scripture Focus

- *Mark 1.14-15*

DID YOU KNOW?

No Photos of Jesus

No place in the New Testament do we get even the slightest idea of what Jesus looked like. There is no reference to his height or weight, the color of his hair and beard, the color of his eyes, anything.

We can only guess. We know he was able to attract crowds and hold them spellbound by his preaching. But this doesn't mean he was physically attractive. It simply means he was a great teacher. We know some of his most loyal followers were women. Does this mean he was handsome? Not necessarily. It does mean he was gentle and kind and treated women with great respect — something that wasn't common for men to do in his time.

He did have to be physically strong, though. He had spent his youth and most of his adulthood in physical labor. He lived out-of-doors most of the time in his public ministry. He'd walk miles each day, often in hot weather and over rough land. But what did he look like?

Because there had been much intermarriage with other peoples in Jewish history, Jews of his time had all kinds of physical features. Some were blond with blue eyes. Some had darker features like brown eyes and black hair. While most men were short by today's standards, some did grow to six feet or more. No help there.

At least we can be certain of this. He dressed, talked, and probably looked like most of the men of his time. If he had been really different (for example, much taller than others) we can be sure it would have been noted in one of the Gospel accounts. This means we can imagine Jesus to look any way we want. It also means that what made him so attractive to all kinds of people were his inner qualities, not his external appearance. There is probably a lesson here for those of us who are so worried about "how we look."

Jesus and the Father

He called a little child over and stood him in their midst and said: "I assure you, unless you change and become like little children, you will not enter the kingdom of God."
(Matthew 18.2-3)

Father Knows Best

In most ancient societies the family structure was patriarchal. That means the father was the unquestioned head of the family. His word was law for his wife and children. Everyone obeyed him, showed him respect, honored him. If someone disobeyed, he was in charge of punishments. Even after the children grew up, they would still go to their father for all the important decisions, and would still obey his every command. For his part, the father was expected to protect his family and provide for them. This was pretty much the case in Jesus' time. It is still the case in many societies today.

In this kind of family, though, the little children were usually given special treatment. They would be loved and cuddled, even spoiled, by the father. They wouldn't be expected to obey all the rules. They weren't given harsh punishments. Only as they grew older were they expected to obey, do their share of the work, keep their distance, and show respect for the father.

The Jewish people came to regard God as their Father. Their image of him was taken from their own earthly fathers. As God's children they were expected to obey him, honor him, and keep their distance. They could expect his punishment if they didn't behave properly.

'Abba' Means Daddy

But when Jesus began his preaching, his approach to God was different. He spoke about God as Father, all right, but not in that formal, even fearful way common in his time. He didn't even use the formal word, father. Instead he used the word *Abba,* which is closer to our own word "daddy," or "papa."

He used the small child's approach. He spoke about God, his Father, as a small child might speak about his daddy, confident that his daddy would do anything he asked, confident his daddy would always protect him and would

Jesus spoke about his Father as a small child might speak about his daddy.

never be mean to him. More important, Jesus encouraged his followers to use the same approach — to become simple, trusting children in their relationship with God.

This was revolutionary! It made many of the Jewish leaders angry. How did Jesus dare to act so special, as if he were on such close, intimate terms with Yahweh, the Lord of Hosts? It was bad enough that Jesus taught strange ideas about the kingdom of God. Now he was teaching strange ideas about God himself.

Of course, we know now what the Jewish leaders didn't know then — that Jesus really is God's special son. But that just makes Jesus' teaching about his Father all the more important to us. Jesus really does want us to be on close, family terms with God. He wants us to be like little children and approach God as our loving Daddy. He wants us to trust God as our loving Daddy, confident he will always protect us and provide for us.

Not Easy to Grasp; Not Easy to Be

But today, two thousand years later, too many Christians still have the old-fashioned idea about God. They fear him, keep their distance from him, approach him only with formal words and rituals. They find it very hard to be childlike and to approach God as their Daddy. "Big people" aren't supposed to act like that. That's too bad because it means they are missing one of the most important things Jesus taught us about his Father. He really is our Father, our Daddy too, and Jesus wants us to approach him that way.

This doesn't mean we can be disobedient or disrespectful. It means our obedience and respect should come from love for our Daddy, not fear of him. To be childlike isn't the same as being childish. To be childlike in relation to God means trust, simplicity, intimacy. To be childish means selfishness, carelessness, thoughtlessness.

This theme of being childlike and of approaching God as our Daddy runs through all of his teaching. But Jesus teaches us something else. All he did and said came from one single motive — to do his Father's will, to bring honor to his Father, to complete the work his Father had given him to do. Jesus never lost sight of that goal. He wanted everyone to know about his Father so they could love him and honor him.

Those who come as little children can expect the Father's love.

What Kind of Kingdom?

You see, Jesus' mission to announce and establish the reign of God is really identical with his goal of leading all people into an intimate, childlike relationship with his Father. The kingdom of God is actually the kingdom of Jesus' Father, his Daddy. The reign of God is actually the reign of Jesus' Father.

That should help us understand more about what kind of kingdom Jesus was proclaiming. It would be a kingdom ruled over by a loving Father, a loving Daddy. In it the members, those who had become as little children, can expect the Father's love, protection, kindness, and forgiveness. In most families the father pays special attention to the weakest, those in most need of help, the sick, those unable to take care of themselves. So it is in the kingdom of Jesus' Father. That's what Jesus said the reign of God would be like. That's how his Father will treat us, his children — if we become like children and accept God as our Father, our Daddy!

The Children's Duty

There's one other thing. True followers of Jesus — those who accept his Spirit as children of the Father — also get caught up in Jesus' mission. Above all, they want to lead others to the Father and to help build the Father's loving reign, the Father's kingdom. Everything else takes second place to that.

Isn't that what the Church is all about? Proclaiming the Father's kingdom and establishing the Father's rule over all of us brothers and sisters in the human family?

So if you want to know how to read the Gospels, how to understand what Jesus was trying to teach, and what his mission was really all about, just remember these things: the kingdom of God is the kingdom of a loving Father, a Daddy in the deepest sense of that word; to enter that kingdom we must become as little children and allow the Father to truly guide our lives.

What Has This Got to Do With Me?

How do you feel about calling God your Daddy? Embarrassed? Awkward? Disrespectful? Comfortable? Why?

What must you do to become more childlike and less childish?

Do you think you could ever get caught up in Jesus' mission to proclaim the kingdom and lead people to the Father?

Review Questions and Activities

1. What do we mean by a patriarchal family?
2. What is so different about Jesus' teaching concerning God the Father?
3. What's the difference between being childlike and being childish?
4. How does Jesus' teaching about his Father affect our understanding of the kingdom of God?
5. How do true followers of Jesus act in regard to the mission of Jesus?

Scripture Focus

- *Matthew 18.2-3*

DID YOU KNOW?

Protector of the Church

We know very little about Joseph, the husband of Mary, and Jesus' foster-father. Most of what we do know comes from a few references in Matthew and Luke. We know he worked with wood. That's what the Greek word for carpenter means. We translate it as carpenter, but it could mean anything from a cabinet maker to someone who made handles for shovels or helped build houses. St. Justin Martyr (c. A.D. 150) said that Joseph probably made ploughs and yoke for oxen. Maybe he did all those things.

We know he was a "just man." In biblical language, to be "just" didn't mean simply that he paid his bills and didn't cheat people. To be "just" meant to be holy, to be obedient to God. We know he had the very special task of caring for and protecting Jesus and Mary, and doing all those things expected of an earthly father. He was probably poor all of his life and had to work — and worry — very much in caring for Jesus and Mary. Since there is no reference to him after Jesus started his public life, it is assumed that he died sometime earlier. We know nothing about his age at marriage or death. We don't know what he looked like. We don't have a single recorded word he spoke.

But we can be sure of this. He must have had a very important influence on Jesus as he grew up. At about the age of eight, Jesus probably began working with him, at least some of the time, in learning the trade. So they spent long hours together. Jesus would observe, as any growing child does, how his father acted, what he said, how he treated his mother, how he treated his neighbors, how he related to God and practiced his religion.

When Jesus began to teach about his heavenly Father, we have every reason to believe he would use experiences from his relationship with Joseph, his earthly father, to help explain what his heavenly Father is like. Forgiveness, patience, concern, intimacy, care, and protection were all qualities he must have observed in Joseph. So even though the Gospels don't tell us much about Joseph directly, Jesus probably told us much about him as he taught about his heavenly Father.

No wonder Joseph is considered one of the greatest saints who ever lived!

Jesus and Miracles

After sunset, as evening drew on, they brought to him all who were ill, and those possessed by demons. Before long the whole town was gathered outside the door. Those whom he cured, who were variously afflicted, were many, and so were the demons he expelled.
(Mark 1.32-34)

That's how Mark describes the close of the *first* day of Jesus' public life. He was making it clear to his readers that the message, which Jesus began to announce that day about the arrival of the kingdom, was backed up with powerful signs from God. That's the basic meaning the Gospel writers gave to Jesus' miracles. They were signs that God's power was in him. They were proofs that Jesus was really God's messenger and that all should listen to him and believe him.

An Old Testament View

Today many people think of Jesus' miracles as proofs that he is the divine Son of God. But the people of Jesus' time who saw the miracles, and even his followers, looked at them differently. They looked at them from an Old Testament point of view. You see, the people considered the Old Testament prophets to be messengers sent by God. One of the proofs that they were really God's spokesmen, and not false prophets, was that God's own power would often flow through them in signs. Many of the Old Testament prophets worked such signs or miracles. Many of these were the same kind that Jesus worked. Read, for example, 2 Kings 4-6. There you will find bread multiplied, cooking oil miraculously increased, lepers cured, poisoned food turned to good food. Elijah even raised a young man from the dead (1 Kings 17.17-24). And note how that passage ends with the woman saying, "Now indeed I know that you are a man of God. . . . The word of the LORD comes truly from your mouth."

So the Gospel writers told the miracle stories against this Old Testament background and compared Jesus' miracles to those of the great prophets of old. For these writers Jesus' miracles were a clear proof that Jesus was sent from God, that he was the Messiah. They came to believe he was God's

Son, however, not from the miracles God worked through him, but from the fact of his resurrection from the dead.

Four Kinds

The kinds of wonders, or miracles, Jesus did, as proof that his message was true, fall into several different groups. The first can be called *spiritual miracles,* and are perhaps the greatest of all. In these miracles we see Jesus touching people's hearts, not their bodies. Persons like Mary Magdalene, whose whole life had been devoted to sin, experience a change of heart simply by being with Jesus and hearing him speak. The same is true of the publican Zacchaeus and many others. His power to drive out demons also showed his spiritual power over Satan's kingdom.

Some of Jesus' miracles of healing might today be called *psychological miracles.* This means he probably cured some people's minds and in this way also cured their physical ills. We know, for example, that when some people experience a great shock or scare or serious guilt, something often goes wrong with their body as a result. Maybe they go blind or lose the use of their legs or can no longer talk. Jesus could inspire in people great confidence, peace, reassurance that they had no need to fear or feel guilty any longer. As soon as they became convinced of that, the physical illness would go away. The illness was really rooted in the mind, not the body. We see some psychologists and religious leaders who can do this same thing. It's just a guess because no one can say for certain, but one example of such a miracle may be Jesus' cure of the paralytic. Chances are his illness was more the result of guilt and fear than any real sickness. Jesus' assurance that he was forgiven freed him psychologically. As soon as this happened the physical side effects left him. (Read Mark 2.1-13.)

But some of Jesus' healing miracles were *physical miracles.* He could directly heal the body, not just the mind. For example, he restored a man's withered arm to wholeness (Matthew 12.9-14). He cured a man blind from

The water jars were filled with water, and the water became wine.

birth, obviously a physical problem, not one in the mind (John 9). He cured from a distance without even coming in contact with the person so he could affect his mind. We see this in the cure of the centurion's servant (Luke 7). He cured lepers whose bodies had been rotting away (Luke 5).

Of course, his greatest physical cures were when he raised different persons from the dead. The first was Jairus's daughter who had only died a short time before (Mark 5). Then he raised up the widow of Naim's son who was being carried to the cemetery. He had been dead for some time (Luke 7). Finally he raised Lazarus who had been dead for several days and was already buried (John 11). God hadn't worked a sign like that through even the greatest of the Old Testament prophets.

Finally, Jesus performed certain *nature miracles*. This means he showed great power over natural forces. He walked on water (John 6), he calmed a ferocious storm with just a word (Mark 4), he changed water to wine (John 2), and he multiplied bread and fishes (John 6).

Faith Is the Greatest Miracle

God had given power to Jesus to drive out demons, to cure the sick, to command the laws of nature to obey as proofs or signs that Jesus really was his chosen one, his special messenger, the Messiah. Why didn't people believe? As we saw in an earlier chapter, people were on guard against false prophets. There were magicians and people who practiced witchcraft who could do some rather amazing things. Many of Jesus' miracles were done in front of small groups of people, so others would have to hear about them secondhand. Some came to see Jesus more out of curiosity than faith. They weren't really looking for the Messiah, just a little entertainment. So they missed the point. Most of all, since the Jewish leaders opposed Jesus, they were able to convince many people that he was indeed a false prophet. They even accused him of witchcraft, saying his powers came from Satan, not God. So we shouldn't be too surprised that the leaders could eventually get many to reject Jesus.

Even Jesus' closest followers, those who saw almost all of Jesus' miracles and heard all his preaching, lost faith for a time after he was arrested. In the long run we don't really know why so many people rejected Jesus despite the signs he provided. We simply know they did.

Not Just for Show

It's good to note a few things about Jesus' miracles. Jesus didn't use the power God gave him for any vain purposes, to attract attention or to overwhelm the people into believing. Most of his miracles were done simply because he felt so sorry for all sick people and their suffering. Often he tried to do the miracles privately so as not to attract a crowd. Sometimes he really didn't want to do a miracle and had to be talked into it. The best example, of course, was at Cana. Another good example is the Canaanite woman from the district of Tyre and Sidon whose daughter was "troubled by a demon" (Matthew 15.21-28).

Also Jesus required faith of a person *before* he would work a miracle, not after it. We read that one time he simply wouldn't do any cures because the people of the town lacked faith. It was his own hometown (Mark 6). He also refused to work any miracles when the Jewish leaders asked him. He knew they didn't believe in him, and any miracles he did for them would be a waste of time, even a misuse of God's power. Jesus never used any of his miraculous powers to help himself escape from his enemies after his arrest or to do any harm to them.

Finally, and this is important for us, Jesus promised that his followers would be given the same kind of powers he possessed if they had strong enough faith. "You can move mountains . . ." (Matthew 21). But they would do them for the same motives as Jesus: to help people believe in Jesus and to help bring peace and healing to the suffering. We do find the Apostles

doing many miracles after Jesus' resurrection and ascension. But they always did them "in Jesus' name" and as a proof that Jesus really is the Messiah. They never did them to attract attention to themselves or to make people think the power was their own. It was God's power being channeled through them because of their faith in Jesus.

Do you realize that the promise to share in Jesus' power still stands today with the same condition — that we have enough faith? Think about that.

What Has This Got to Do With Me?

Do you think people really could work miracles in Jesus' name today if they had enough faith? Do you think you could?

What do the stories of Jesus' miracles prove to you? What should they prove?

What spiritual miracle would you like Jesus to work for you?

DID YOU KNOW?

Demon Possession

Possession by evil spirits seemed quite common in Jesus' time. Many people have tried to explain such possession in natural ways — epileptic fits, insanity, and the like. But even today we have cases that seem to make sense only in terms of demonic possession. You probably don't remember it, but a very popular movie a few years back, called *The Exorcist*, dealt with demonic possession. It was based on a true story. (Don't be fooled, though, by many of today's popular movies on the topic; they are based on fiction.)

But the fact remains, there is much evidence that demonic possession still takes place today.

The Church still has a rite for casting out demons. It is called exorcism, but the rite is not used very frequently. For one reason, the Church is always slow to draw the conclusion that there is a demonic possession just because there are some strange things happening. But once it has decided that it is facing a real case of possession by an evil spirit, the rite is used. Only specially trained and appointed priests, noted for their holiness, are allowed to perform the rite. They are able to drive out the evil spirits in Jesus' name because Jesus still shares this power with his Church.

Review Questions and Activities

1. How did the people of Jesus' time approach miracles?
2. Name the groups of miracles described in the chapter.
3. Give an example of each taken from the Gospels.
4. What did Jesus require before he would work a miracle?
5. Why did Jesus promise to share his powers with his followers?
6. Name and give an example of the four kinds of miracles Jesus performed.

Scripture Focus

- *Mark 1.32-34*

Unit Review

1. Describe the events surrounding the conception and birth of John the Baptizer.
2. Describe the three temptations experienced by Jesus.
3. Give an example of each of the following forms of Jesus' teaching method: parable or story, use of an event taking place, personal example, a formal talk.
4. Why is Jesus' teaching about God's mercy so important to the kingdom?
5. How does Jesus' teaching about his Father affect our understanding of the kingdom of God?

Some Words to Know

ADULTERY • The act of a married person having sexual relations with a person other than his or her spouse.

BAPTISM • Sacrament of the Church which initiates new members into the Christian community, freeing them from Original and all sin.

EXORCISM • The act of driving out an evil spirit.

IDOLATRY • The worship given to a person or thing which properly belongs to God.

KINGDOM OF GOD • The reign or authority of God over the hearts and minds of his followers.

MARTYR • A person killed for religious beliefs. The word is from the Greek meaning "to witness."

MERCY • A characteristic of God which allows him to love us despite the fact that we have offended him.

MIRACLE • An event, unexplainable by the laws of nature, which indicates divine intervention.

MISSION • The task of each Christian to bring others to know Jesus and his Church. From the Latin meaning "to be sent forth."

MONASTIC LIFE • A manner of living together under a common rule, secluded from the world in order to pursue spiritual perfection in the service of God.

PARABLE • A comparison or story from everyday life that helps us understand a deeper truth.

PATRIARCHAL FAMILY • A family in which the father rules over everyone in an absolute way.

REPENT • To change one's life, to reform.

RITUAL • A form for carrying out religious rites and ceremonies.

SYNAGOGUE • A gathering place for the Jewish people for religious services, used by those Jews unable to get to the Temple.

TEMPTATION • Enticement to do wrong by promise of pleasure or gain.

UNIT 3

Followers, Faith, and the Future

INTRODUCTION

This unit deals with the followers of Jesus, those who came to believe in him and especially those he chose to be his helpers. They were, of course, the Twelve Apostles. They had much to learn before they were able to carry on the mission Jesus would give them. Also important were the women who followed and cared for Jesus. Of all the women who followed Jesus none is more important than Mary, his mother. There will be a special chapter devoted to her, her role in Jesus' life and mission, and her role in the Church today.

All Jesus' followers need faith. To nurture faith we need prayer. Jesus taught his followers how to pray — and he teaches us how to pray. Faith must lead to good works or it is dead. Jesus taught his followers — and us — what he meant by good works. This is the moral teaching of Jesus.

Finally, faith involves the future. Jesus taught his followers about the future and how to deal with it.

As you read this unit, try to imagine yourself as one of those chosen by Jesus to be a special follower. How might you have reacted as Jesus taught you how to pray, to act, to approach your future?

Jesus and the Apostles

He then went up the mountain and summoned the men he himself had decided on, who came and joined him. He named twelve as his companions whom he would send to preach the good news; they were likewise to have authority to expel demons.

(Mark 3.13-15)

In Jesus' time when a person began to preach he could usually get people to listen, at least for a while. John the Baptizer was a good preacher. Many would listen, maybe out of curiosity, and then go back to their old lifestyle. Others would listen, agree with what John said, and then go back home determined to practice what the preacher had taught them. Still others would not only agree but become disciples — students of the preacher. That means they would not only try to practice what John said but follow him around as much as possible so they could learn more.

Many Are Called . . .

It was much the same with Jesus. When he began to preach some would listen for a while. Maybe they would even follow him around for a day or two. Then they would drift away and return to their old habits.

Some would listen and experience a real change of heart and mind. They might have to get back home and to work, but they would go back changed. They followed Jesus' way even if they could not follow him physically. Jesus also attracted disciples — people who were so changed by his preaching that they followed him everywhere, at least as often as they could. Maybe they would go back home for a while to take care of things, but as soon as they could they would return to Jesus so they could hear more of his teaching.

Some became disciples simply because they became convinced on their own that Jesus was special.

Some became disciples because a friend convinced them that Jesus was special. That's how Peter first became involved. That's how Nathanael got involved. (Read John 1.35-50.)

And some became disciples because Jesus personally invited them. Matthew is a good example. (Read Mark 2.13-18.)

By whatever means, a following of disciples soon gathered around Jesus. They didn't spend every minute with Jesus, but they did spend every minute they could. We assume they'd go back home when they had to — many were married and had family duties — but they would return at the first chance. Jesus went back to some of them himself and invited them to follow him more closely — to become real disciples, not just part-time disciples. (Read Luke 5.1-11.)

Few Are Chosen . . .

Gradually Jesus gathered an inner band of disciples. As Luke tells us, many gave up everything just to be with him. Jesus must have made some impression to get people to give up EVERYTHING! In time Jesus chose, from all these disciples, twelve men whom he made his Apostles. Apostle means messenger, a person sent to represent the sender, and having almost the same power or authority as the sender. Today it would

be like being an ambassador for the president. Before Jesus made his choice of the Twelve he spent the night in prayer (Luke 6.12-13). Remember that.

What We Know

We really don't know that much about the people Jesus chose. We know even less about *why* Jesus chose them. But here are some things we do know about the men Jesus chose to take his place and build the Church that has lasted for almost two thousand years:

• Eleven of the twelve were from Galilee, Jesus' own area. Judas, the betrayer, was possibly from Carioth, a town in Judea in southern Palestine.
• Three were related to Jesus, probably as cousins: James the Less, Jude, and Simon the Zealot.
• Five were fisherman: Peter and Andrew, James and John, Philip.
• One was a tax collector, Matthew, who was also called Levi.
• There were three sets of brothers: Peter and Andrew, James and John, James the Less and Simon the Zealot.
• Only one had any position of authority, Matthew, the tax collector. But that was not the kind of authority that impressed the Jews of Jesus' time.

Can you name all twelve? It is no surprise if you can't. But think about this. Of all the people alive and available when Jesus was doing his mission, they were the ones he chose. Of all of them, the two most people could name today are Peter and Judas — and both betrayed him in their own ways! John and Matthew we know because they wrote Gospels. The

others? Each is mentioned in the Gospels in one way or another. Usually it is in a situation that makes them look bad. For example, we know about Thomas because he was a questioner and doubter — the original doubting Thomas.

Philip doesn't seem to be in touch with what Jesus is about (John 14.8-9). John and James have bad tempers, so much so that Jesus nicknamed them the sons of thunder (compare Mark 3.17 and Luke 9.51-56).

Judas was a thief and worse (John 12.6).

All but John went into hiding once it was clear Jesus would be executed. In other words, his chosen, special followers were not always very courageous.

Poor Judge of Character?

At first glance, you might think, not a bad group, not a terrific group. So why did Jesus make such choices? Here are some reasons:

• Jesus' standard for judging people was the kingdom of God that he was preaching. In that kingdom the only important people are those who can *admit* they need help. All but Judas could do that.

• Jesus picked people who were not happy with the way things were. Nobody keeps something the way it is if it is not okay. In other words, the people he chose for a special job were the ones willing to take a risk and change.

• Jesus picked people, not because they were perfect, but because they were willing to try. If Jesus had picked only the most perfect people, we ordinary types would be afraid to try to follow Jesus. Instead he picked people who were slow at learning, people who were vain, who argued about who was the most important, people who could be cowardly at times. Yet all but one turned out to be saints — through Jesus' help and influence. That should give us hope that we can actually become saints too, no matter what weaknesses we have right now.

They Met the Challenge

Once Jesus chose the Apostles, they went everywhere with him. They would listen, observe and remember. Often Jesus took them aside and taught them special things he didn't tell the crowds. He even gave them some "practice missions" to preach the good news of the kingdom. In short, Jesus was preparing them for the day when they would have to take over for him. The results of their preaching have lasted almost two thousand years, so they must have learned their lessons well, despite their weakness. Of course the Holy Spirit had something to do with their success.

Jesus has disciples today.

In this band of Apostles several seemed to be special friends of Jesus. He appointed Peter to be the head of the group — and of the future Church. So Jesus included him in some special situations, like when he raised Jairus's daughter from the dead and when he was transfigured. Jesus also had to be hard on Peter at times in order to prepare him for his special role. James and John and Peter's brother, Andrew, were also included in some of these special occasions. Those four were also the very first to follow Jesus. Philip was among the first also, and seemed to be special to Jesus.

All the Apostles, however, must have felt pretty good about themselves when Jesus chose them from all the others. They must have enjoyed some of the attention they received simply by being close to Jesus and being recognized as his Apostles wherever they went. The early days must have been exciting, full of surprise and adventure. Like many others, they, at first, thought Jesus would found an earthly kingdom and that they would have key positions of honor and power in it. Sure, it was hard work and hard living. They were constantly on the move, eating whenever they could, sleeping out of doors, spending long periods of time away from home and family. But it was worth it. They knew Jesus was a prophet. They admired him. They loved him. And they knew he loved them! It never really entered their minds that Jesus might one day be killed for his preaching — even though he kept warning them. Even though they followed Jesus loyally for almost three years, it still took his death and resurrection to help them finally understand what he had been teaching them.

What Has This Got to Do With Me?

Today every Christian is supposed to be a disciple of Jesus. How do you measure up?

Has a friend or relative ever "brought you to Jesus" or helped you come closer to him? Have you ever done the same for a friend?

Can you guess how you might react if Jesus ever chose you to be his special friend? Are you sure he hasn't?

DID YOU KNOW?

About the Apostles

Here are some random facts and traditions about the Apostles: James the Greater, brother to John, was the first Apostle to be martyred. He was beheaded around A.D. 42-44 in Judea by King Herod.

Greater and lesser are titles used to distinguish between two Apostles with the same name. They mean older and younger, not better and worse.

Jude (Thaddaeus) has become the patron saint of hopeless cases.

Tradition says that all the Apostles except John died as martyrs. We can be sure they were all persecuted for their preaching.

Thomas's nickname was *Didymus,* which means twin in Greek, so he was probably a twin.

Matthew seems to be the only one who had some education and was probably wealthy. Tax collectors were usually well-off and had to have some education to get the position.

Simon the Zealot belonged to a radical party before he was called by Jesus. The Zealots were in favor of violent revolution to drive out the Romans.

Matthew, John, and Peter all wrote parts of the New Testament.

Tradition tells us John never married. It may be that most of the others were married. We are sure Peter was.

Review Questions and Activities

1. What's the difference between disciple and Apostle?
2. Name the Twelve Apostles.
3. How do we benefit by the fact that Jesus chose some weak people as his Apostles?
4. Who seemed to be Jesus' special friends among the Apostles?
5. What did all the Apostles but Judas have in common?

Scripture Focus

- *Mark 3.13-15*

CHAPTER 14

Jesus and Women

His disciples, returning at this point, were surprised that Jesus was speaking with a woman.

(John 4.27)

No Women's Lib Here

Women had it tough in Jesus' day and age. Here are just a few of the customs in practice then. Women weren't expected to go out in public alone. They certainly weren't supposed to speak to strange men. That's why the disciples were surprised when they found Jesus talking to the Samaritan woman. If women went to the well, for example, they were expected to go as a group. They were expected to wear veils.

Women were not allowed to speak up at synagogues or other public places. In the Temple there was a special place for women, further removed from the Holy of Holies. A family was considered blessed by Yahweh if a male child was born. If a female child was born, it wasn't quite a curse, but it was a bit of bad luck. This was partly because boys were expected to take care of their parents in old age. Girls would marry and become the property of another family. In the legal sense that's what women were — property.

On the other hand, it wasn't quite as bad as it sounds. Jewish men showed great respect for their wives and daughters, protected them, provided for them. Within the home the women pretty much had the run of things. So women weren't exactly slaves. But they

Holy Land mother and child.

didn't have the freedom or the opportunities of men in Jesus' time.

Jesus Was Different

When Jesus began to preach he attracted large numbers of women, as well as men. It seems quite a few women became disciples, just like the men who followed him devotedly. Women weren't as free to do this since they had to stay nearer to home. But they did follow him. (Read Luke 8.1-3.)

Because of the customs of the time, they couldn't get involved in the ministry like men. But they did help Jesus in many ways — behind the scenes. They would provide and cook food and in other ways take care of daily needs. In the process some became very close friends of Jesus — and his most loyal followers. By accepting them, he broke many of the customs of the time. This was a scandal to the Jewish leaders and even to many of his male disciples.

Jesus publicly talked with women. He associated with them freely. He allowed them to be his followers and to listen to his teaching. On a number of occasions he showed them special treatment and consideration. He was gentle and kind to them. No wonder they became such loyal followers.

Special Treatment

If you check you'll find that a large number of Jesus' miracles involved women. We know, for example, that it was Jesus' mother who convinced him to change water to wine at Cana. The first person he raised from the dead was the daughter of Jairus. Even as he was on his way to raise the girl he cured a woman with a hemorrhage (Mark 5.25-35). The second person he raised from the dead was a widow's son — because he felt sorry for her.

Women served as examples in many of his teachings: the widow's mite, his treatment of the woman taken in adultery, the repentance shown by Mary Magdalene, the faith of Martha, and the devotion of her sister, Mary.

Clearly, the kingdom was intended for both men and women.

Weaker Sex?

In fact, women in general come off looking a lot better than men in the Gospels. When the Apostles — with the exception of John — went into hiding after Jesus' arrest, the women stayed by him, even helping him along the Way of the Cross. They stood by until his death and then assisted in burying him. They were the first to find the empty tomb. And it was to a woman that Jesus first appeared after the resurrection — not to the Apostles. In fact women were the first to announce the good news: He is risen! They were sent to bring it to the Apostles.

In our day, the role women played in

the life and teaching of Jesus might not seem significant. But we should remember that in Jesus' time his teaching and his treatment of women was revolutionary! Jesus had come to bring freedom to the oppressed, the poor, the defenseless. In Jesus' day, women were oppressed. These are the very ones for whom the kingdom is intended.

So we shouldn't be surprised that women saw hope in Jesus' words and in his treatment of them. It's no wonder they would become some of his most loyal, devoted, and courageous followers. Also, Jesus said the kingdom belonged to the little ones, the children, the simple, and the humble. Given their low status in society, it was not hard for women to see the value of these virtues.

To a large degree that is still true today. Society continues to nuture an attitude that makes it easier for women than for men to be religious and to adopt the childlike qualities necessary to enter the kingdom. Men have somehow gotten the idea that to be religious is to be weak or cowardly.

As the women who stood by the cross have shown us, however, to be religious and childlike is anything but cowardly. It is probably the most courageous thing a person can do, man or woman.

The Gospel is for all — women and men equally. No preferences. No biases. Jesus came to liberate all from our sin and weaknesses.

What Has This Got to Do With Me?

Who do you think are more courageous when it comes to religion, boys or girls?

Have you ever been teased for your religion?

What do you think is "a woman's place" in the Church? Why?

Review Questions and Activities

1. Why was it considered bad luck to have a girl child instead of a boy child in Jesus' time?
2. List some ways women were restricted in Jesus' time.
3. What was so appealing to women in Jesus' message?
4. In what ways did women behave better than men in the Gospel story?
5. Is Jesus' message more appropriate for women than for men?

Scripture Focus

- *Luke 8.2-3*

The Twelve accompanied him, and also some women who had been cured of evil spirits and maladies; Mary called the Magdalene, from whom seven devils had gone out, Joanna, the wife of Herod's steward Chuza, Susanna, and many others who were assisting them out of their means.

DID YOU KNOW?

Women and the Church

Throughout the history of the Church we find women playing key roles alongside men. We can start with Mary, Jesus' mother. We've just seen that women were an important part in Jesus' public life. In the early Church it was much the same. Groups of women often accompanied the Apostles on their preaching journeys, helping them and caring for them. Some women held positions of authority in the local churches. Women accepted martyrdom as frequently and as bravely as the men during the persecutions. We find women saints mentioned frequently through the centuries, although not as frequently as male saints. Women have been missionaries, teachers, and founders of religious communities and hospitals. Jesus really has been an "equal-opportunity employer."

Except in one important area. There's no hard evidence that women ever served as ordained priests. There's nothing in Scripture that strictly forbids it. It is a custom, dating back to Jesus' appointment of the Apostles. The custom has never changed. As a result, men have always been in the key positions of official authority in the Church.

There has been much discussion of the role of women in the Church. the Church's tradition remains unchanged concerning ordaining women, but other options are being studied. One is the diaconate. The discussion will no doubt continue.

CHAPTER 15

Jesus and Mary

When Elizabeth heard Mary's greeting, the baby leapt in her womb. Elizabeth was filled with the Holy Spirit and cried out in a loud voice: "Blest are you among women and blest is the fruit of your womb."

(Luke 1.41-42)

Just the Facts

Over the centuries so many legends and superstitions about Mary have developed it can be hard to get an idea of just who she is and the real role she played — and plays — in the history of salvation. So let's begin with some of the few facts we really do have concerning her. Most of these come from the Gospels themselves.

We know she was born of the tribe of Judah and of the royal house of King David. David was her ancestor and thus Jesus' ancestor. Earliest tradition tells us her parents were Ann and Joachim, but we know little about them. She probably grew up in Nazareth in Galilee. That's probably where she first met Joseph. She probably became engaged, or betrothed, to him when she was about fifteen, the customary age. The engagement was probably arranged by the parents of both Joseph and Mary, again the custom of the day.

At that time, to be engaged was much like being married. The man and woman could live together as husband and wife, but the formal marriage ceremony wasn't celebrated until the husband could set up a household, support his wife and bring her to live with him. So it wouldn't have been any scandal if Mary had become pregnant before the formal marriage ceremony.

We know she became pregnant with Jesus through the Holy Spirit. But Joseph didn't know that, at least, not at first. He knew he wasn't the father. So he had a right to be concerned and worried until God revealed the truth to him.

We know that Mary went to a cousin, Elizabeth, who was already six months pregnant with John the Baptizer, and stayed three months or until the birth of John. It's safe to imagine she helped Elizabeth, already quite old, during those last months of pregnancy.

A Mother's Role

We know she and Joseph had to go to Bethlehem just about the time she was due to give birth and that Jesus was born in less than ideal conditions in an old stable or cave-stable. The event attracted the attention of local shepherds. Mary didn't know just what

all this meant, but she did know her baby would have a special role to play in God's plans for Israel.

We know Joseph decided to hide the family in Egypt for a while because he had reason to fear for the child, whom they named Jesus, as Yahweh had commanded.

Later they settled in Nazareth, their original hometown, and set up housekeeping. The only thing we know for sure from that period was their trip to Jerusalem for the Passover when Jesus was twelve (Luke 2.41-52). We can only presume they lived much like anyone else in Nazareth during that time. This means Joseph would work at his trade. Mary would attend to the house. She would be responsible for Jesus during his early childhood. Joseph would assume a greater role as

Jesus grew older, teaching him a trade and helping him associate more with the men of the village.

They were a religious family, much like the others in the village. They followed the Covenant Laws and read the Scriptures. They taught Jesus to do the same. They would attend the synagogue services on the Sabbath and, when possible or when they could afford it, go to Jerusalem during the great feasts.

We don't know what Mary's friends thought of her. But it's doubtful Mary's looks or actions differed from any of the other housewives and mothers who would gather at the well to fetch the day's supply of cooking and washing water. Tradition tells us, however, that she led a sinless life, so acquaintances must have known she was a unique woman.

In her heart she knew she and her son and her husband were different somehow — with a special blessing and a special call from Yahweh. But only time unfolded to her just how blessed she really was and just what that special call would cost her. She had to learn what God was asking of her, much as the rest of us do.

A Follower Like the Others

After Jesus left home to begin his public ministry, there are several other Scripture references to Mary. We find her at the wedding at Cana, an invited guest of the family. From that story it is clear Jesus loved his mother and had a hard time refusing her anything she asked — the same kind of devotion

Devotion to Mary has taken many forms.

we'd hope every son would show his mother.

She appears as part of the crowd on at least one occasion and seeks to see her son personally. So she must have followed him at least during some of his journeys. But we find her in the background, asking no special treatment, making no special demands on Jesus or his time. In other words, once Jesus left home and began his ministry, she didn't try to interfere.

Later we find her in Jerusalem for the Passover feast when Jesus is arrested and executed. As a brokenhearted mother she stays with him right up to his death. While hanging on the cross, Jesus entrusts her to John's care. We know she is part of the community gathered after the resurrection. But virtually nothing is said of her after Pentecost.

What's So Special?

If we stay with just these Scripture references, what can we say about Mary? From Luke's story of the Annunciation we can see that she was both humble and obedient, faithful and courageous. Her "yes" to Yahweh's request that she become the mother of Jesus was a "yes" like no other in history. It was a greater act of faith than even that of Abraham, the father of faith. By it she entrusted her whole self, body and soul, and her entire future to God and whatever he willed for her.

The rest of the story simply tells us how she kept that promise totally and without complaint. She never wavered in her trust. She daily followed whatever it was God asked her to do, knowing that somehow it would help complete God's plan and bring about his kingdom. When you stop to think about it, faith, or trust, is precisely what God asked of her.

Trust, when Joseph was considering leaving her. Trust, when they had to travel to Bethlehem just when she was due to give birth. Trust, when she ended up having to give birth in a cave. Trust, when they had to go into hiding in Egypt. Trust, when the long years of the day-to-day routine in Nazareth seemed to indicate anything but a great future for her son. Trust, when he left home and began preaching. And most of all, trust, when she stood there watching him die by inches, his whole ministry and all that it seemed to promise dying with him. Yet finally, trust, as she awaited the Spirit's descent after Jesus' ascension.

So who is Mary, really? She is the mother of Jesus. She is a woman with the greatest of faith and trust in God's love. She is humble, obedient to God's gentle rule in all things. She lived simply, a woman like all others of her time, but she loved greatly and she suffered greatly in response to God's call to her.

And Jesus gave us this woman to be our mother too!

What Has This Got to Do With Me?

Does your life *seem* unexciting to you? Does that mean that God doesn't have anything special for you?

What kind of trust is God asking of you?

Do you ever take advantage of the fact that Jesus gave Mary to you as a mother?

Review Questions and Activities

1. Who were the parents of Mary and what was her family background?
2. What were the key events in Mary's life before Jesus began his public life as described in Scripture?
3. Describe Mary's role during Jesus' public life.
4. Based on Scripture, how would you describe Mary?

Scripture Focus

- *Luke 1.41-42*

The Annunciation.

DID YOU KNOW?

Mother Most Holy

There are three days on which the Church celebrates Mary's special place in God's kingdom and her special role in our salvation.

The feast of the Immaculate Conception, celebrated on December 8, commemorates the fact that Mary was preserved from original sin from the first moment of her conception. No other person ever born was so preserved. The present form of the feast dates from 1854, when Pope Pius IX defined the dogma of the Immaculate Conception, but the belief has been documented as early as the eighth century.

The feast of the Annunciation, celebrated on March 25, commemorates the announcement to Mary by the Archangel Gabriel that she was to become the mother of Jesus. This feast has been observed almost universally throughout the Church since the seventh century.

The feast of the Assumption, celebrated on August 15, commemorates the taking into heaven of Mary, body and soul, at the end of her life on earth. This was proclaimed a dogma by Pope Pius XII in 1950, but was celebrated as a feast of the Church as early as the seventh century.

There are other days on which Mary is also honored. One is called Our Lady of the Rosary, which is celebrated October 7. The Rosary is one of the time-honored prayers of the Church. Its origin dates back to the twelfth century, and in its present form to the fifteenth century. The words of the prayer are rooted in Scripture and tradition. The main elements of the Rosary are (1) meditation on fifteen mysteries, or events, in the lives of Jesus and Mary, and (2) recitation of a number of decades of Hail Marys along with various prayers: Apostles' Creed, Our Father, Glory be to the Father, and others, depending on custom. (See pp. 192-195.)

From the Church's earliest days, Mary has been honored with various titles. They have come down to us in the form of the Litany of the Blessed Virgin. Here are some of the titles:

- Holy Mother of God
- Mother of Our Savior
- Virgin Most Faithful
- Comforter of the Afflicted
- Queen of Peace

The complete litany is found on page 196-197.

Jesus and Morality

After he had sat down his disciples gathered around him and he began to teach them.

(Matthew 5.1-2)

Time-out for a review.

√ Jesus was a teacher and prophet.

√ His key message was about the arrival of the kingdom and the nature of the kingdom.

√ The flip side of this message about the kingdom was the message about the Father — our Father. After all, the reign of God and the reign of our Father are the same.

√ His power to do miracles was a proof that he really was sent by God.

√ His selected Apostles were less than perfect, but they, except for one, served loyally through their struggles.

√ Jesus was revolutionary when it came to respecting women. Mary, his mother, was very special and deserves our love and devotion.

So far that's what we saw we can learn from Jesus and the New Testament.

Nothing New?

But what did Jesus teach about sin? About what is good?

The fact is, when it came to morality Jesus taught very little that wasn't already taught in the Old Testament. He said he didn't come to destroy the Law, but to fulfill it (Matthew 5.17-20). For example, Jesus is probably most quoted as teaching the two "great" commandments of love: love God above all and love your neighbor as yourself. Actually these weren't new commandments. They can be found in the Old Testament. (Read Deuteronomy 6.4ff., and Leviticus 19.18.) Much of what Jesus taught about lying, adultery, stealing, for example, is all straight out of the Old Testament and was considered law by the Jews of his day. Even the beatitudes, some of Jesus' most profound sayings about how to live and what to value, can be found in the Old Testament, at least, in their root form. So what did he teach about morality that was new?

Everything New!

Jesus didn't really teach so much that was new. He just taught it differently. To put it another way, Jesus taught people to go beyond the letter of what was said in the Old Testament. He taught them to go beyond external practices. He taught them — and us — to discover the *spirit* of the laws. For example, it isn't enough to avoid murder. How many people ever think seriously of committing murder? What we need to do is avoid anger, cutting words, verbal "punches and stabs." It isn't enough to avoid adultery. We must avoid even thinking about it.

It isn't enough to love your neighbor. You should love your enemy too and even do good to those who are mean to you! So Jesus didn't teach new laws. He taught a new way to practice them. He presented the ideal. That's what we find in his Sermon on the Mount. The most complete version is in Matthew 5-7. As you read those chapters you find that he is calling us to the ideal, not just the minimum.

Another thing we find throughout the Gospels is that Jesus is opposed to phoniness — to people who keep laws just to impress others and win their praise. That was something that most angered him about the Pharisees. They could talk a good game and even put on a good show. But they were using the Law to their advantage, not as a guide for loving God and neighbor.

Who Is My Neighbor?

The most revolutionary part of Jesus' moral teaching was how he answered the question "Who is my neighbor?" Read Luke 10.25-37, which includes the parable of the Good Samaritan.

In Jesus' time it was common practice to be good to family members, to friends, to fellow Jews. Those were neighbors. But that's where the Law stopped. You didn't have to be good to non-Jews, especially Samaritans, to Gentiles, to enemies, social outcasts and sinners. They were not neighbors. But Jesus saw it differently and said so. For him everyone is our neighbor. Friends and family, sure, but also

Who is your neighbor?

enemies, outcasts, and even sinners. Everyone is a child of God, called and invited to the kingdom. We should show concern and respect and extend our hand to help anyone in need, not just a select few.

That was revolutionary moral teaching: just to be good to everyone since everyone is our neighbor. As we said earlier, that was how Jesus treated lepers, publicans, prostitutes, Samaritans. That was how he treated women, the poor, the weak, and the unimportant people in his society.

Hard to Take

This upset the Jewish leaders and the upper-class types. They thought it was enough to follow the externals of the Law, pay the temple tax, say their prayers, and offer the required sacrifices. They didn't like it when Jesus told them they should also be good to lepers, to publicans, to the beggars and the poor who crowded the streets in their dirty clothes. That was too much. They'd have to change too much.

Jesus really didn't single out many particular sins as being worse than others. After all, sin is sin and all of it is bad. In fact, Jesus spent most of the time teaching his disciples about doing good rather than teaching them to avoid particular sins. His emphasis was on the positive. But one sin in particular he did warn against more than most. It was the sin of scandal.

That is, he warned his followers to be careful not to give bad example and lead others away from the kingdom (Matthew 18.7).

He aimed this warning especially at the Jewish leaders. They had a lot of influence over the people. For them to give bad example was doubly bad. That is true for us too. We've been lucky enough to learn about Jesus from our childhood.

So three unique characteristiacs of Jesus' teaching are: strive to be perfect rather than just doing the minimum; obey the spirit of the Law, not just the externals; and most importantly, apply it to everyone, since everyone is our neighbor.

What Has This Got to Do With Me?

Do you shoot for the ideal or the minimum when trying to follow Jesus?

Do you try to follow the spirit of the law or the letter of the law?

Do you think of EVERYONE as your neighbor?

Review Questions and Activities

1. What are the two "great" commandments?
2. Where do you find these in the Old Testament?
3. In what three ways did Jesus teach morality differently?
4. How did the Jewish leaders react to his teaching on morality? Why?
5. Why was Jesus so opposed to scandal or bad example?

Scripture Focus

- *Matthew 5.17-18*

Do not think that I have come to abolish the law and the prophets. I have come, not to abolish them, but to fulfill them. Of this much I assure you: until heaven and earth pass away, not the smallest letter of the law, not the smallest part of a letter, shall be done away with until it all comes true.

DID YOU KNOW?

Neighbors

Many of *your* neighbors today are poor and hungry. Here are just a few facts:

- Each year 15 to 20 *million* people die as a result of hunger and starvation.
- That's 41,000 people every day!
- That's twenty-eight every minute, twenty-one of whom are children!
- One out of every three people on earth goes to bed hungry at night.
- We could prevent hunger in the world with 25 billion dollars. That's about what the armed nations spend on weapons and military supplies every seventeen days! It would cost people of non-hungry nations about eleven dollars per person per *year*!

How much money have you spent on junk food and video games or movies this month?

Can you imagine what Jesus might ask you to do to help these neighbors of yours, children of the Father just like you?

Jesus and Prayer

> *One day he was praying in a certain place. When he had finished, one of his disciples asked him, "Lord teach us to pray, as John taught his disciples."*
>
> (*Luke 11.1*)

Among all the things Jesus taught us — by word and example — prayer is probably the most important. Let's start with the example of prayer Jesus gave us.

Public Prayer

First, he prayed with the community at the times the community usually prayed. In other words, he had a public or community prayer life.

We find him going to the synagogue on Sabbath days. We find him in the Temple. He made a special effort to attend the feast days there and to celebrate them in the way the community celebrated them. The name for this kind of praying is *liturgical* prayer. Jesus prayed this way with the community. (That's what liturgical prayer is — praying with the people.)

Here's an example from the Gospels where Jesus prayed this way:

> *Shortly afterward they came to Capernaum, and on the Sabbath he entered the synagogue and began to teach.*
>
> (*Mark 1.21*)

At Mass we are a praying people.

Spontaneous Prayer

Another way Jesus prayed is sometimes called "spontaneous" prayer. This means he simply prayed in his own words because he felt like it or because he thought that's what was needed. Maybe you or your parents do this at meals sometimes. Here is an example of this kind of prayer:

They then took away the stone
and Jesus looked upward and said:

> *"Father, I thank you for having*
> *heard me.*
> *I know that you always hear me*
> *but I have said this for the sake of*
> *the crowd,*
> *that they may believe that you*
> *sent me."*
>
> (John 11.41-42)

A monk in private prayer. Contemplative orders provide men and women unique opportunities for private prayer.

Prayer in Private

A third way Jesus prayed was in private. He went away by himself. Remember the desert experience of Jesus? He seemed to do this whenever he could. Here's an example:

> *Rising early the next morning, he went off to a lonely place in the desert; there he was absorbed in prayer.*
>
> (Mark 1.35)

Some Guidelines

If Jesus spent so much time in prayer and taught his followers to do the same, what did he teach about praying? We can summarize it in four key points.

• *Pray with confidence.* One of the main themes of Jesus' preaching was that God is our Father. Our Father wants us to be happy. He'll never refuse us if it is for our good (Luke 11.9-13).

• *Don't give up.* Too many people give up after praying a few times. Jesus taught that we should keep praying. Often, if our prayers aren't answered right away it's because we don't have enough faith. Just as often it's because what we are praying for isn't good for us. If we keep praying God will answer our prayers — even if we don't know what we should be praying for, or why (Luke 11.5-8).

• *Pray always.* God is always in touch with us and our needs. We should stay in touch with God in the same way. It doesn't mean we should spend all our time in church in some kind of formal prayer. It means we should listen for God in daily situations. If we have the right intentions, most of what we do is a kind of prayer. Even homework is a kind of prayer if we do it as a way of showing God how much we want to do what is right (Luke 18.1-8).

• *Don't be showy.* Jesus made a big point about not being a show-off when it comes to prayer. Praying is talking with and listening to God. It's not for impressing others about how good we are (Matthew 6.5-9).

Some Motives

Why did Jesus pray? He taught us four reasons or purposes for praying. The first is obvious. We pray to God when we need help. We call this *prayer of petition.* Second, we pray to God to express our sorrow and seek God's forgiveness when we've done something wrong. We usually call that *prayer of sorrow,* or *contrition.* Another reason for praying is to thank God, to express our gratitude for all he does for us in general, and for the times he answered our prayers of petition. This is called *prayer of thanksgiving.* The fourth reason for praying is simply to give God praise for being God. This is called *prayer of praise* or *adoration.* Since Jesus never sinned, he never really had to use the prayer of sorrow, but we can find him praising his Father,

thanking him, and asking his help.

All prayer has this in common: to seek God's will for us and to have the strength to accept his will.

Our Father. . .

Once when his disciples asked Jesus to teach them to pray, he taught them what we now call the Our Father (Luke 11.2-4; Matthew 6.9-14). It's considered the perfect kind of prayer because it has all the qualities we talked about above. The opening words, "Our Father" (that is, "Daddy") suggest our confidence and closeness to God. The phrases "hallowed be thy name, thy kingdom come," and "thy will be done" are expressions of praise. They are also petitions. But they don't ask anything for us. They show us what we should really be asking for, what is most important: the Father's kingdom and his plans. Next are petitions for ourselves. We ask for "daily bread," or for today's needs. We ask for forgiveness. But it's based on our willingness to forgive those who do wrong to us. If we aren't ready to forgive others, we have no right to ask God to forgive us. That's important to remember. Finally we ask our Father to protect us from the worst kind of thing that could happen to us — falling into sin or Satan's control, the opposite of God's rule or kingdom.

If we really understand these phrases in the Our Father and mean it when we say them, we are putting into practice just about everything Jesus ever taught us about prayer. The Our Father is truly Jesus' prayer — and the prayer of all his followers.

What Has This Got to Do With Me?

What would it take for you to "pray always"?

On a scale of one to ten how do you rate your confidence when you pray?

Do you remember to praise and thank God, not just to ask him for things?

DID YOU KNOW?

A Praying People

If you need proof about the importance Jesus placed on prayer, all you have to do is look at his followers over the centuries. In the Acts of the Apostles, a good record of the Church in earliest times, it seems the Apostles and other followers prayed in just about every situation: to give praise, to ask for help, to seek guidance, to say "thank you." One thing they had learned, though, was to pray in Jesus' name, as he taught them. It seems the Father can't refuse Jesus anything.

We see the same thing in most of the epistles. Often they begin and end with a prayer of praise, thanksgiving and petition.

Many followers of Jesus imitated his desert experience. They dedicated their whole lives to praying. Many still do. Thousands of monks and nuns all over the world are devoting their lives to praying in "desert" monasteries and convents.

Every week millions of Jesus' followers gather to celebrate and pray. We call it "going to Mass." All four kinds of praying in the most perfect form are contained in the Mass.

Also, prayer groups are popular today. People gather to read the Scriptures and to pray together, sometimes spontaneously, sometimes in more formal ways. Chances are there are such groups in your parish. Some of the most popular books among Jesus' followers today are the ones dealing with how to pray.

So praying is alive and well two thousand years after Jesus' death and resurrection. It must be important. Try it out for yourself.

Review Questions and Activities

1. What three kinds of prayer did Jesus teach by his example?
2. What qualities should our prayer have?
3. What four reasons, or purposes, should we have for praying?
4. Explain why the Our Father teaches us everything we should say and do when we pray.
5. What key lessons can we learn from the lives of monks and nuns?

Scripture Focus

- *Luke 11.1-2*

Jesus and the Future

"Stop worrying, then, over questions like, 'What are we to eat, or what are we to drink, or what are we to wear?' The unbelievers are always running after these things. Your heavenly Father knows all that you need. Seek first his kingship over you, his way of holiness, and all these things will be given you besides. Enough then, of worrying about tomorrow. Let tomorrow take care of itself. Today has troubles enough of its own."
(Matthew 6.31-34)

We worry a lot. It seems that we never have enough control over the things in our lives. We're afraid of how things are going to turn out.

Jesus tells us there are better things to think about. Since we are human, we need to think about food, clothing, a place to live. Jesus was a human being too, and had to think about such things. (In fact, he thought about it for five thousand people on one occasion.)

But Jesus is trying to tell us something about perspective, about priorities. In other words, he's saying let's put first things first.

How Did He Do It?

Our focus here is on how Jesus viewed the future. We know he experienced a call by his Father at his baptism. As his mission continued, he would have to explain and re-explain his teachings. He would confront all types of people, some of whom would attempt to sabotage his efforts. The immensity of his mission must have weighed upon him more heavily as time passed. He knew the Scriptures and what the Scriptures said about the Messiah. So he realized that eventually he would be killed and that the Father would raise him from the dead. Scripture contained those kinds of prophecies.

It was clear that the kingdom he proclaimed wouldn't be perfectly established in his own lifetime. (No doubt it became more obvious as time passed.) That's why he chose his Apostles and began to train them to be able to carry on his mission after he was gone. Also he began preparing the Apostles by telling them about his death and resurrection. He did this a number of times. (Read Mark 8.31-33, 9.30-32 and 10.32-34.)

But it seems they never really understood what he was telling them. Maybe, like any of us, they just didn't want to think about something so scary and unpleasant. So even though Jesus had warned them, his death — and his resurrection — still came as a surprise to them.

The Kingdom and the Future

The kingdom would not be established perfectly in Jesus' own lifetime. Jesus even taught this. He taught that the kingdom would develop slowly, like a tiny seed growing into a tree (Matthew 13.31-32). He taught that evil would remain alongside of good in the kingdom until the very end of time (Matthew 13.24-30). He warned his followers that they'd have to suffer like him in order to bring about the reign of God (Mark 13.9-13 and Mark 8.34-38). The Apostles and other followers didn't fully understand this kind of teaching either, until after he was killed and was raised from the dead. Only then did it begin to make sense to them.

Much of what Jesus said about the future, then, was based on his awareness of what the prophets before him had said about the Messiah, his mission, and the results of his mission. Jesus knew with absolute certainty that the kingdom would eventually be established in all its perfection. But he also knew this would take a long time and that there would be an ongoing struggle between good and evil in the process. He knew that at the end of time he would return to rule over the kingdom alongside of his Father. Basically that's what he taught his followers about the future.

Stay alert! Be ready!

When the End?

But Jesus never taught just when the end would come and the kingdom would be perfected. He did talk about that end time and what it would be like, but he never gave an exact time. That decision belonged to his Father, and even Jesus wasn't free to talk about it. We can read what Jesus did teach in Mark 13.24-31. Matthew and Luke say almost the same thing in their Gospels. Matthew also gives us Jesus' description of the Last Judgment. Read it in Matthew 25.31ff.

Jesus also warned about the coming destruction of Jerusalem and the Temple. He foretold all the terrible suffering the people would experience during that time. Because this prophecy is written right before his teaching about the last days, people sometimes get the two predictions mixed up. The destruction of Jerusalem and the Temple happened in A.D. 70, when most of the Apostles were still alive. Obviously the end time hasn't happened yet.

'Tomorrow?'

In just about every generation, though, people think their own time will be the end. Jesus' warning about wars and rumors of wars, false prophets, strange natural events on earth and in the sky don't really seem to be that much help. In just about every period in history many of those things seem to have taken place. The time we live in right now seems to be full of those kinds of signs.

Because Jesus didn't tell us just when the end will occur, he also gave us some important advice: Stay alert! Be ready! Don't let day-to-day concerns and distractions fool you. Live as though the end would come tonight. That's the message contained in his Parable of the Ten Virgins and the Parable of the Silver Pieces. You can read them in Matthew 25.1-30.

When the Gospels came to be written, much of what Jesus warned us about was already happening. For example, the Romans had already destroyed Jerusalem and the Temple before the Gospels took written form. Persecutions were taking place throughout the Roman Empire, much as Jesus had warned. So these predictions and advice must have been a big help to the Christians of that time. It helped them understand what was happening and how important it was to keep up hope. The predictions and advice can be just as helpful to us today.

A Summary

In summary, then, here's what Jesus teaches us about the future:

- We can be sure that the kingdom will be perfectly established and that Jesus will come again.

- But it will be a slow process and we have no way of telling just when the end time will occur.

- Even though the reign of God will gradually spread throughout the world, there will always be evil forces trying to keep it from spreading.

- As followers of Jesus we need to stay alert.

- As followers of Jesus we can expect people to give us a hard time and make fun of us simply because we are trying to follow Jesus.

All earthly things decay, but we do not know when the end will come.

- As followers of Jesus we can remain confident about the future no matter how tough things get in the present.

There's one other thing to keep in mind in talking about Jesus and the future. Jesus knew he would eventually be tortured and executed. We really have to admire the way he didn't let that knowledge interfere with his mission. He kept teaching and helping people right up to the last. He didn't try to hide. He didn't go around feeling sorry for himself. Like any of us, he must have had feelings of fear, and his future must have worried him.

We can learn from that. It's okay to have feelings of fear and to worry about the future sometimes. But, like Jesus, we shouldn't let these feelings prevent us from doing what is right in the present. Like Jesus we should have confidence in the Father. Though things can get tough at times, the Father will never abandon us.

What Has This Got to Do With Me?

Do you worry too much about your future?

Would you be ready if Jesus returned today?

How are you helping to spread the reign of God?

DID YOU KNOW?

O Jerusalem! Jerusalem!

A Roman army led by Titus destroyed Jerusalem and its Temple in A.D. 70, just as Jesus had predicted. The Jews had tried several rebellions before the Romans did this. After the destruction, all that was left standing in the whole city was one of the walls of the Temple. It is still there today and is called the Wailing Wall. Jews still go there to weep and pray. For a long time no Jews were even allowed to go into Jerusalem after the city was rebuilt. Those who survived the destruction fled throughout the empire. Since many had become Christians, this disaster actually helped to spread the Gospel.

Over the centuries Jerusalem was held by various foreign powers. But as Christianity grew, many Christians would go there to visit the places where Jesus had been. Many shrines and churches were built there and throughout Palestine. For centuries the Moslems held the Holy Land, as Christians call it today. They didn't like Christians and tried to keep them out. In the Middle Ages crusader knights tried to recapture the Holy Land from the Moslems. They were successful for a while. In modern times the British ruled the Holy Land until after the Second World War. Then thousands of Jews from all over the world came to live there and they eventually succeeded in creating an independent state of Israel again. But no new Temple has ever been built in Jerusalem.

Review Questions and Activities

1. How did Jesus know so much about his own future?
2. How did he describe the future of the kingdom?
3. What did he teach his followers about their own future?
4. Did his followers understand Jesus?
5. When were Jerusalem and the Temple destroyed as Jesus had predicted?

Scripture Focus

- *Matthew 6.31-34*

Unit Review

1. What is the difference between a disciple and an Apostle?
2. What was so appealing to women in Jesus' message?
3. What were the key events in Mary's life before Jesus began his public life?
4. In what three ways did Jesus teach morality differently?
5. What four reasons, or purposes, should we have for praying?
6. How did Jesus describe the future of the kingdom?

Some Words to Know

ANNUNCIATION • The feast that celebrates the event in Mary's life when she was asked to be the mother of Jesus.

APOSTLE • A special representative or messenger for Jesus.

ASSUMPTION • The feast that celebrates Mary's being taken into heaven, body and soul.

CONTRITION • A feeling of true sorrow.

DISCIPLE • A student or one who follows another's preaching.

FORMAL PRAYER • Prayer with definite words and/or actions.

IMMACULATE CONCEPTION • The feast that celebrates the fact that Mary was preserved from original sin, from the first moment of her conception.

LAST JUDGMENT • The final determination of a person's everlasting destiny.

LITURGICAL PRAYER • The prayer of the community. Religious rites used for public worship.

PETITION • The act of asking for something.

PRAISE • In prayer, the act of responding to the supremacy of God.

PRIVATE PRAYER • Prayer by oneself.

SCANDAL • Bad example in thought, word, or deed.

SORROW • The expression of sadness over a deed done.

SPIRIT OF THE LAW • Hidden meaning of the Law.

SPONTANEOUS PRAYER • A prayer made up "on the spot."

THANKSGIVING • The act of gratitude.

UNIT 4

No Greater Love

INTRODUCTION

In this unit we now focus on the central events of Jesus' life and mission: his early success, the growing opposition, his triumphant entry into Jerusalem on Palm Sunday, his Last Supper with his Apostles, his arrest, trial and execution — and Easter Sunday!

Jesus' ministry is usually considered in two parts: his Galilean ministry and his Jerusalem ministry. His Galilean ministry deals with his early ministry; his Jerusalem ministry deals with his last days, or the events of what we have come to call Holy Week.

In this unit we are confronted with mystery:

• The mystery of evil which drove people to reject Jesus and eventually to kill him.

• The mystery of God's love, mercy, and fidelity which led Jesus to undergo torture and death to redeem the very people who rejected him.

• The mystery of God's power, which overcomes evil and death and restores Jesus — and us — to life.

Try to imagine yourself as a pilgrim in Jerusalem during that last week of Jesus' life. How might you have reacted to the events that took place both before and after Jesus' execution?

Jesus and His Ministry in Galilee

Jesus returned in the power of the Spirit to Galilee, and his reputation spread throughout the region. He was preaching in their synagogues, and all were loud in his praise.
(Luke 4.14-15)

People who study the Gospels usually consider Jesus' ministry in two parts. The first is his ministry in Galilee. The second is his ministry in Jerusalem. During the three years Jesus taught, he actually wandered throughout the whole country. On a couple of occasions he even went outside the borders for a short time. But he spent the largest part of his time in Galilee. Only toward the very end of his life did he focus all his attention on Jerusalem.

As the quote above shows, Jesus began his ministry in his home territory of Galilee. He did most of his teaching in Galilee and worked most of his miracles there. While he had disciples from all over, the majority came from Galilee. All of the Apostles except Judas came from Galilee.

Accepted at First . . .

At first Jesus was very popular. The people loved what he taught and the way he taught. They were thrilled by his miracles. He drew a huge crowd anywhere he went. Right from the beginning, though, the Jewish leaders were nervous about him and tried to find fault with him in front of the people. Some of the people, too, disagreed with him — even in his home town (Mark 6.1-6). Jesus was never one hundred percent successful. But in the beginning he was popular and many people did accept his teaching about the kingdom and about his Father. Gradually, though, the Jewish leaders gave him more and more problems. Just as bad, it seems many of the people never really understood that the kingdom he proclaimed was spiritual, not political. They followed him for the wrong reasons. They kept hoping he'd be a political leader. They misinterpreted his miracles as proofs that he could easily overthrow their enemies rather than overthrow Satan.

Jesus Reacts

As this happened you can see Jesus becoming upset with them. You might say he was losing his patience with the people for their lack of real faith. For example, read Matthew 11.16-24.

Those are hard words. But they are justified. Jesus also becomes more and more frustrated with the Jewish leaders. They were one of the reasons the people were failing to appreciate what he was teaching and doing. He begins to speak out against them more and more. For example, read Matthew 15.1-20.

We also find Jesus beginning to withdraw from the people so he can spend more time training his Apostles. Once he went to the area of Tyre and Sidon, which was actualy outside Jewish territory (Matthew 15.21).

Who Am I?

About this time Jesus finally asked his Apostles what they thought of him. He never asked them that before. This is when Peter gives his famous answer, "You are the Messiah," and Jesus appoints him as head of his Church. This had to be reassuring to Jesus (Read Matthew 16.13-20). At least his Apostles seemed to be catching on, even if they had a long way to go. From that time on we begin to find a shift in Jesus' teaching and in his ministry. He now begins to look to Jerusalem and the work he must do there — the work of salvation. He begins to teach his Apostles about his coming death and resurrection. We've already seen they didn't fully understand these predictions, but Jesus kept warning them. He tried to prepare them in other ways too, like the Transfiguration (Matthew 17.1-9). In other words, once Jesus was convinced he wasn't going to win over all the people in Galilee or the Jewish leaders, he began to focus on the Passion he knew was to happen.

Jesus walked through the Galilean countryside to teach . . .

The Turning Point

The real turning point in Jesus' Galilean ministry, though, seems to come when he begins to teach about the Eucharist. We can read the whole story in John 6.25-69. Do it now. John tells us that from then on many of his disciples no longer walked with him. But when Jesus asked his Apostles if they were going to leave too, we once more hear Peter speaking out for the group to reassure Jesus: "Lord, to whom shall we go? You have the words of eternal life" (John 6.68).

It wasn't just the teaching about the Eucharist that turned people away. It was more like the last straw. People were becoming disappointed in Jesus for some time already. The people wanted freedom from Rome. Jesus offered freedom from Satan and sin. Many of the poor and powerless wanted to become rich and powerful, so they could get revenge on the "big shots" of their time. Jesus taught that we should pay more attention to spiritual treasures, that we should forgive our enemies, that we should seek to serve rather than rule over others.

. . . and around the Sea of Galilee.

Put simply, their desire to "get their share" of the pie prevented them from hearing Jesus' message. They were too concerned about getting even. Also, what Jesus taught sounded too good to them — promises of a perfect society, a kingdom under God. On the other hand, Jesus' teachings were too hard. He talked about turning the other cheek, being blessed for being poor, trusting in him more than in their own mothers and fathers — or even themselves. He promised too much, and he asked too much. The people in Galilee — at least, many of them — couldn't rise to that kind of faith. So they returned to their old ways, to wait for the "true Messiah."

So Jesus turned to Jerusalem. The lack of faith there, as we'll see, was for different reasons.

A Lesson Here

But we can learn from the people of Galilee. They were Jesus' kind of people. A number were related to him through Mary and Joseph. Many were the rejects, outcasts and powerless people he most wanted to tell about the Good News of the kingdom. In a real

Who is leading you?

sense, they, like the shepherds in Luke 2.8, heard the Good News first. What lesson is there for us?

First, we can pick up the wrong kinds of values. We can get wrong ideas of what will make us happy. When someone tells us what we really need, we don't believe him. We can be misled by supposed leaders who seem to know it all. Some popular entertainers, even friends or peers, might do that to us.

Anyway, what Jesus most asked of the Galileans was for them to believe in him, to trust him. By his words, his actions, and his miracles he thought he had given them good reason to do so. But only a few really did — at least, at first. So he turned to Jerusalem and a showdown with the Jewish leaders.

What Has This Got to Do With Me?

How do you feel about what Jesus taught us about the Eucharist?

Do you think Jesus asks too much of you?

Where are you getting your values and how do they line up with those Jesus teaches?

Who is leading you?

Review Questions and Activities

1. How did the people react when Jesus first started teaching?
2. How did the Jewish leaders treat Jesus?
3. What did Peter answer when Jesus asked the Apostles who they thought he was?
4. Why did many people stop following Jesus?
5. How did the people react when Jesus taught about the Eucharist?

Scripture Focus

- *Luke 4.14-15*

DID YOU KNOW?

Arm Twisting

We've said the Jewish leaders — at least some of them — opposed Jesus from the beginning and used their influence to keep others from following him. One thing they could do to put pressure on the people was threaten to put them "out of the synagogue" (John 12.42-43).

Ever since the Babylonian Exile in the sixth century B.C., when the Temple was first destroyed, Jews would gather in a local meeting hall or synagogue to pray, read Scripture, and hear their teachers. Even after they returned to Israel and rebuilt the Temple, almost every town still kept it's own synagogue. Going to the Temple, except for those who lived in or near Jerusalem, was a special treat. Maybe they did it once a year; maybe even once in a lifetime, for the Jews who lived outside the country. But there was always the synagogue. It was within walking distance. It was where your friends gathered. It was where you could pray, hear God's word, and have it explained to you.

So to be told you could no longer go to the synagogue was like being told you were no longer a member of the community. Friends would no longer talk to you or do business with you. Your family would get the same treatment. To be out of the synagogue was to be "excommunicated." For simple people their whole life meant being accepted by their neighbors and going to the synagogue. Being put out was about the worst thing that could happen to them.

That's why the Jewish leaders could put pressure on people. To follow Jesus would mean being put out of the synagogue!

We can't be too hard on people in Jesus' time who didn't seem to remain faithful to him. In one sense, to be a follower of Jesus, the Son of God, is much easier today than when Jesus, the carpenter's son from Galilee, called for followers.

Jesus and His Jerusalem Ministry: Palm Sunday

Then Thomas said to his fellow disciples, "Let us go along (to Jerusalem) to die with him."
(John 11.16)

There are two parts to Jesus' mission. On the one hand, he was sent to proclaim the kingdom of God and call people to enter it. That's what his Galilean ministry was about. On the other hand, Jesus was sent to *conquer the forces of evil* which were opposed to the kingdom. That's what Jesus' Jerusalem ministry was all about.

From the Beginning . . .

From the very beginning the political and religious leaders opposed Jesus. So after he completed his mission of proclaiming the kingdom, mostly in Galilee, he turned toward Jerusalem to do battle with his enemies and the forces of evil they represented. He confronted the leaders face to face, although he knew they would kill him. He would not win by force of arms. Instead he would conquer death itself, the ultimate weapon of evil. After the leaders killed him there was nothing more they could do to Jesus. When he rose from death they knew they had lost. So the Jerusalem ministry is the story of Jesus' last days, the final battle, and it is completed with his resurrection. It is a story full of drama. As we have seen in an earlier chapter, it is the turning point in history.

'Lazarus, Arise . . .'

The story actually begins when Mary and Martha call Jesus to help their brother Lazarus. The Jewish leaders had been threatening Jesus for some time. But Jesus avoided them and Jerusalem as much as possible. He still had some work to do proclaiming the kingdom and training his Apostles. When he decided to go to Lazarus' home, just a few miles from Jerusalem, it was the beginning of the end. He was going into the enemy's home territory. That's when Thomas said, "Let us go along, to die with him."

The Apostles were beginning to sense the danger Jesus had been talking

A modern Palm Sunday procession.

about. You can read the story of the Raising of Lazarus in John 11. This miracle, the greatest Jesus had done so far, was performed in the shadow of Jerusalem with a large crowd present. It sent shudders of fear through the Jewish leaders. It seemed everyone would follow Jesus now. That's when the leaders made up their minds, once and for all, to have him killed. Up to now they had only talked about it. Now they began to make serious plans.

After he raised Lazarus from the dead Jesus once more withdrew for a short while. But the stage was set. When he returned to Jerusalem the next time, it would be for the final confrontation.

Palm Sunday

Jesus picked that time carefully. He returned at the time of the Jewish Passover, their biggest feast of the year. People from all over the world would be there. Since Jesus always went to Jerusalem for the Passover, the crowds would be looking for him, especially now that the story of raising Lazarus from the dead spread among them. There was an air of excitement everywhere. Of course, the Jewish leaders were on the lookout. Jesus knew that during this Holy Week, he would become the new Passover.

Then, word went out. Jesus and his disciples were coming into the city from Bethany. Crowds went out to greet him, to get a glimpse of this holy man, this miracle worker. They wondered, "Perhaps, he really is the Messiah." He passed along the road, with the crowds lining both sides. Someone started chanting: "Hosanna! Blessed is he who comes in the name of the Lord! Blessed is the king of Israel." It was from Psalm 118 and all devout Jews knew it. Soon everyone was chanting it, waving palm branches and throwing them in his path. Some used their cloaks the same way. As they got caught up in the spirit of the event, it became like a royal welcome. It was as if Jerusalem and all Israel were coming out to greet their king. Little did they realize how true that was, or how they would be treating their king a few days later. Once again the Jewish leaders panicked. But they couldn't do anything then. The crowd would never let them arrest Jesus at that time.

We can read all about this in John 12. You should already be familiar with it from the Palm Sunday reading we hear each year. In a sense it was the finest hour of Jesus' ministry, the one time the people really treated him with the honor and praise he deserved. But he wasn't fooled by it. He knew how fickle people could be. He knew what was ahead for him.

A Den of Thieves

Jesus, buoyed by the reaction of the crowd, went up to the Temple. Money changers and merchants had set up shops inside the Temple to do business with all the pilgrims who were in the city. Jesus went into a just rage. He drove them out, knocking over their tables as he did. It must have been a sight. No one dared stop him. Besides, what he was doing was right. The Temple was God's house, not a cheap market. The Jewish leaders should have done that long ago and the people knew it. The Jewish leaders' anger mounted. But they had to wait for the right moment before they could get their revenge.

After his triumphal entry into Jerusalem, and after throwing the money changers out of the Temple, Jesus spent some time teaching. Then in the evening, he went back to Bethany. He was a guest at Lazarus' house. It seems he didn't stay overnight in Jerusalem because it would be too dangerous. Sometimes he'd spend the night camping out on the Mount of Olives. At other times he'd stay with Lazarus, or another friend. Mary anointed his feet at Lazarus' house. You can read about that in Mark 14.1-9.

The rest of the week Jesus came to Jerusalem each day to teach. He gave some of his most powerful lessons during that time. We'll review them in the next chapter. And he continued doing verbal battle with the Jewish leaders. The tension kept growing.

The Leaders

Before we go on with the story, though, we should say a little more about the Jewish leaders. First, not all of them were bad. Jesus even had some disciples among them, although they kept it secret. Nicodemus was such a person. He probably tried to warn Jesus of the plots against him.

Secondly, among the leaders who opposed Jesus, some were very sincere. They truly feared that Jesus was a false prophet who was leading the people astray. They had good intentions.

Others were definitely blinded by their pride, their vanity, their desire for power. These were the real enemies of Jesus. They represented the forces of evil. How people could become so blinded is still something of a mystery — and a lesson in just how powerful evil can be.

What Has This Got to Do With Me?

Thomas said he was ready to die for Jesus, but he later fled. What do you promise Jesus?

How would you deal with honors like those Jesus had on Palm Sunday? How important are honors to you?

What could keep you from believing in and following Jesus?

 Jerusalem today.

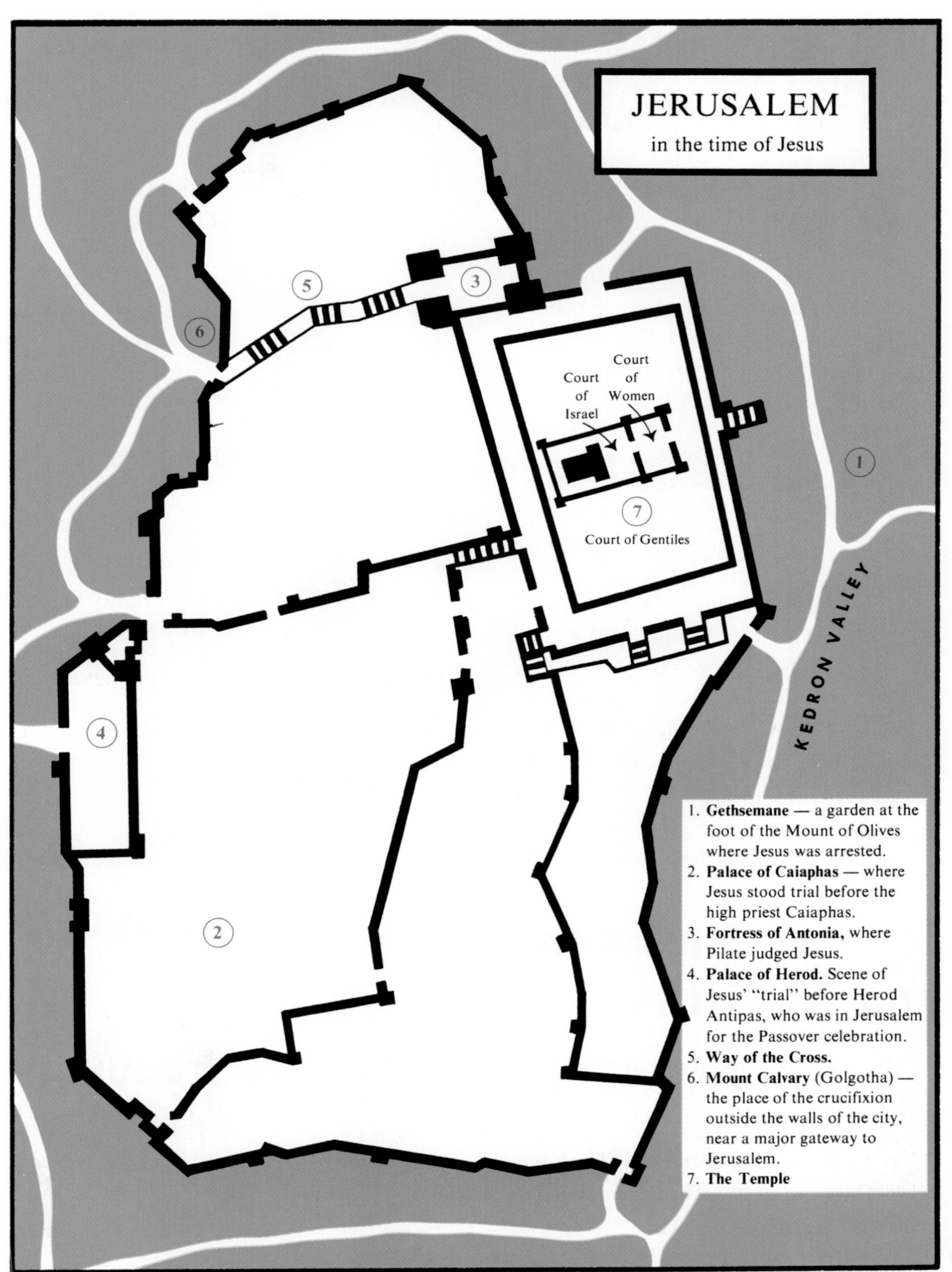

JERUSALEM
in the time of Jesus
Court of Israel
Court of Women
Court of Gentiles
KEDRON VALLEY
1
2
3
4
5
6
7
1. **Gethsemane** — a garden at the foot of the Mount of Olives where Jesus was arrested.
2. **Palace of Caiaphas** — where Jesus stood trial before the high priest Caiaphas.
3. **Fortress of Antonia,** where Pilate judged Jesus.
4. **Palace of Herod.** Scene of Jesus' "trial" before Herod Antipas, who was in Jerusalem for the Passover celebration.
5. **Way of the Cross.**
6. **Mount Calvary** (Golgotha) — the place of the crucifixion outside the walls of the city, near a major gateway to Jerusalem.
7. **The Temple**

DID YOU KNOW?

Sacramentals

When we celebrate Palm Sunday, we take the blessed palms home and keep them in a special place as a reminder of Jesus and what he did for us. Because they have been blessed as symbols related to our salvation story, they are no longer simply branches. They are sacramentals.

A sacramental is an object that is blessed by the Church and has some special religious meaning. Basically, sacramentals are reminders. They remind us of what God does for us and how we should respond to God.

For example, holy water is a sacramental. It is water blessed by the Church to remind us of our baptism. When we use it we recall how God saves us and also how we should act as God's children.

Other sacramentals include the crucifix; the ashes used on Ash Wednesday (ashes from burning last year's blessed palms); and the oil used in the sacraments of baptism, confirmation, holy orders, and anointing of the sick.

The rosary and blessed medals and statues of the saints are other examples of sacramentals.

Sometimes people have thought that sacramentals have magical powers. They've tried to use them in superstitious ways as if they were a spiritual rabbit's foot or a four-leaf clover. Sacramentals aren't magic. They're reminders of God, and their value as reminders is rooted in faith, not magical powers.

Review Questions and Activities

1. What are the two parts of Jesus' ministry?
2. Who was Lazarus?
3. Why did Jesus choose the Passover as the time to confront the Jewish leaders?
4. What is a sacramental?
5. How does your parish celebrate Palm Sunday?

Scripture Focus

- *John 11.16*

Jesus and His Jerusalem Ministry: The Confrontation

"Woe to you scribes and Pharisees, you frauds! You shut the doors of the kingdom of God in men's faces, neither entering yourselves nor admitting those who try to enter."
(Matthew 23.13-14)

No Debate Team

After Palm Sunday Jesus came to Jerusalem and the Temple each day to teach the people. The Jewish leaders followed him everywhere and kept challenging him, hoping to trick him into saying something they could use as an excuse for arresting him. First, they challenged his authority (Matthew 21.23-27). But Jesus turned the question around and trapped them in their own game. Next, they asked him about paying taxes. They really thought they had him that time. Taxes were a hot issue. The Jews hated paying taxes to the Romans. Also they weren't allowed to use Roman money to pay the Temple tax. It had the emperor-god's picture on it. That's why there were money changers in and near the Temple. They'd change Roman money to Jewish money — at a nice profit for the service. Jesus gave the famous answer, "Then give to Caesar what is Caesar's, but give to God what is God's." You'll find the story in Matthew 22.15-22. Next they challenged him about the resurrection. Once again Jesus put them in their place (Matthew 22.23-33).

The people were amazed at how easily Jesus handled these questions. The Jewish leaders became more and more embarrassed. But they kept trying. Next, they asked him about the commandments and which was the most important. That's when he taught the two "great" commandments of the Old Testament (Matthew 22.34-40).

Opportunity to Teach

Jesus took advantage of these situations to teach the people who gathered. He warned them about the false teaching of the Jewish leaders. That's the real point behind the

parables of the wicked tenants and of the wedding banquet (Matthew 21.33—22.14). He warned the people that they shouldn't make the same mistakes the leaders were making by failing to accept Jesus. This running battle between Jesus and the Jewish leaders finally reached its peak. Jesus no longer minced words. He went on the attack. You'll want to read this passage now. Chapter 23 of Matthew is devoted to it.

Strong Language

Here are some of the highlights. First, we see that Jesus isn't out to destroy our need for people in authority. He says we should obey the rules of legal authorities, no matter how bad the rulers might be in their own lives. That's the message in Matthew 23.1-3.

But often he calls the leaders hypocrites and show-offs. He calls them frauds! Several times! He calls them blind guides! He calls them a vipers' nest and a brood of serpents! That was a *real* insult. In Jewish theology Satan disguised himself as a serpent to mislead the people. This comparison wasn't missed by the Jewish leaders or by the people.

These are the words of an angry man! They are the words of a man who has been deeply hurt. He is being rejected by the very people who should have been his most faithful followers. He is saying these things about the leaders who have all the power. These are words of a man who has "pulled out all the stops." The people have to know, even though he's going to get killed for telling them. There is nothing more frustrating or upsetting than watching people you love do things that will hurt them — no matter how hard you try to warn them. That's the real meaning of Jesus' cry, "O Jerusalem, Jerusalem murderess of prophets and stoner of those who were sent to you! How often have I yearned to gather your children, as a mother bird gathers her young under her wings, but you refused me" (Matthew 23.37). Those words say what parents often feel when their children ignore their advice.

This is the background for Jesus' predictions about the destruction of

Confrontation today!

Jerusalem and also the end of the world. We talked about this in Chapter 18. But we can see how serious Jesus was when he said these things. He knew his own death was near. Time was running out. No more time for patience. He was giving it, as we say today, his "best shot."

Superbowl Week?

You should be able to see why Jesus' Jerusalem ministry was so important. In terms of what was happening, what went before it and what he was trying to do, this was Jesus' week of triumph. That's why we remember this week in the Church as Holy Week, the most important week in the year.

Each time the Jewish leaders challenged Jesus and lost, their anger grew. Finally they found a weak link, Judas Iscariot. It was like breaking the enemy code. He agreed to tell them when and where it would be safest to arrest Jesus. The price was right. Only thirty pieces of silver. Not a bad price to pay for protecting your lifestyle — and killing the Savior of the world.

Again we have to deal with the mystery of evil. How could such intelligent people fail to see the goodness of Jesus? How could people dedicated to religion actually plan to kill someone, anyone? How can people get so trapped by wanting to control and wanting to be respected that they'd kill an innocent person to keep that control and respect?

The power of evil is real. Only Jesus challenged it and won. Thank God he did. That's what we celebrate in the Eucharist. We'll talk about that next.

What Has This Got to Do With Me?

Did you ever try to challenge what Jesus — or your religion classes — try to teach you? On what topics?

Would Jesus be upset with you right now? What can he praise you for?

Does anything in Matthew 23 apply to you?

Review Questions and Activities

1. What did the Jewish leaders try to do every time Jesus taught?
2. How did Jesus handle these questions?
3. What was the real reason Jesus was angry at the Jewish leaders?
4. What are some of the names Jesus called the Jewish leaders?
5. How did the Jewish leaders finally react?

Scripture Focus

- *Matthew 23.13-14*

DID YOU KNOW?

Tithing Is Not New

In almost every religion the faithful are encouraged to give alms for the care of the poor and to donate money to help pay for the costs related to the religion: upkeep of the Temple or sacred buildings, support for the priests or other people in charge of the religious functions and buildings.

It was no different in the Jewish religion. Giving alms was encouraged; it was even considered a duty to share your goods with those in need. In the society of Jesus' time many poor people depended on alms for their survival. Jesus challenged showiness in giving alms but he always encouraged generosity.

At that time there was a regular Temple tax all devout Jews were expected to pay. It went for the upkeep of the Temple and the support of the priests and Temple attendants. Occasionally we find Old Testament stories of wicked priests who used the donations of the faithful for their own purposes instead of the support of the poor or the upkeep of the Temple. This kind of injustice was always considered a very serious sin. To stress this point we sometimes find God directly acting to punish such wicked men as an example of how bad he thought it was. A good example of this kind of wickedness can be found in 1 Samuel 2.12-17. Eli's sons were eventually punished for their sins, but such evil practices did continue from time to time right up to Jesus' day.

Tithing (to give one tenth) was a practice in the Old Testament. People were expected to give one tenth of their wealth to Yahweh for the help of the poor and the support of the Temple. Often the poor tried to do this while it would be the rich who cheated. Jesus accused the Jewish leaders of his time of this kind of cheating.

In any event, as Catholics, we too are expected to give alms to the poor and to donate regularly to the support of the Church. People sometimes complain about this. Some people ignore their duty. Others donate but are showy when doing so. Times don't seem to change much, do they? But as Catholics you are expected even now to help the poor and support the Church. Maybe you can't afford much now, but like the widow Jesus praised, your generosity is never forgotten by God.

CHAPTER 22

Holy Thursday

On the first day of the feast of Unleavened Bread, the disciples came up to Jesus and said, "Where do you wish us to prepare the Passover supper for you?" He said, "Go to this man in the city and tell him, 'The Teacher says, My appointed time draws near. I am to celebrate the Passover with my disciples in your house.' "

The disciples then did as Jesus had ordered, and prepared the Passover supper.

(Matthew 26.17-19)

The Passover celebration focused on a special meal. This meal recalled the meal the Israelites ate on the evening Yahweh freed them from slavery in Egypt. It was a religious celebration. This meal had rules about what and how to eat, what songs to sing, and what psalms to pray. These rules can be found in Exodus 12. This was the most important feast of the Jewish year. Pilgrims from all over the world came to Jerusalem.

A Passover celebration today.

A Different Mood

Usually the meal and the overall feast were a joyful time — solemn but joyful. After all, the Jews were celebrating their salvation, their "Fourth of July." But as Jesus and the Apostles gathered, the mood was more tense. The Apostles didn't help matters. They began arguing with one another about who was going to sit in the preferred places. Can you imagine that — after spending three years with Jesus? Jesus gave them a good bawling out. But then he did something so beautiful we still celebrate it today on Holy Thursday. Rather than simply tell them to seek the lower places instead of the places of honor, he showed them. He took on the task usually done by servants in those days. He washed his disciples' feet! It was the custom for guests to have their feet washed when they arrived at the host's house. But not by the host. Jesus, the teacher, the master, the Messiah, took on the role of a servant for his Apostles. They were embarrassed, especially Peter. Jesus finished this lesson by instructing the Apostles, saying, "As I have done, so you must do" (John 13.15). They never forgot it.

He washed his disciples' feet.

After that, things settled down and much of the meal proceeded according to custom. But then Jesus began to do new things.

> *During the meal Jesus took bread, blessed it, broke it, gave it to his disciples. "Take this and eat it," he said, "this is my body." Then he took a cup, gave thanks, and gave it to them. "All of you must drink from it," he said, "for this is my blood, the blood of the covenant, to be poured out in behalf of many for the forgiveness of sins."*
>
> *(Matthew 26.26-28)*

More Than Table Talk

Also during and after the meal Jesus talked as he had never talked before. He talked about his Father. He talked about his love for his Apostles. He talked about what was soon going to happen and about the future (John 14-17). All this confused the Apostles. They realized this meal and Jesus' actions and words were special, but it was only later that they would begin to understand what it all meant.

- Jesus was establishing the Eucharist.
- Jesus was establishing a New Passover and a New Covenant with God.
- Jesus was establishing a means to be with us throughout history.
- Jesus was establishing a meal as the sign of the kingdom he proclaimed, a meal where everyone was equal and everyone shared and cared for one another. This was a sacred meal which would continue Jesus' sacrifice through all of time.

That's why he commanded the Apostles to share the bread and the cup, his Body and Blood.

His Hour

The meal ended and they all went out to the Mount of Olives, just outside Jerusalem. They often camped there. Judas knew that and had told the Jewish leaders.

Jesus knew his final hour was near. Like any of us, he was frightened. So frightened that he literally sweat blood. He would have liked to find an easier way out, and he told his Father that. But he prayed for strength and he made his decision to follow the Father's will to the bitter end. In his struggle Jesus had asked some of his closest friends to pray with him. They kept falling asleep! He had to face the struggle alone.

Mount of Olives today.

By the time the soldiers and the Jewish leaders came to arrest him, Jesus was at peace. He was calm, in total control again. He would remain obedient to his Father even to the moment of his death.

Arrested!

Things moved quickly. Peter made a futile effort to rescue Jesus, but Jesus offered no resistance. They tied him up and led him away for a "trial," the first of several. Most of the Apostles fled. Peter and John followed from a distance and ended up in the courtyard of Annas. That's where the soldiers took Jesus. That's where Peter denied he ever knew Jesus — three different times!

This first "trial" was more like a preliminary hearing. The Jewish leaders were trying to come up with some charge they could use to justify putting him to death. That's some justice! First they arrest Jesus, then they try to find a reason for the arrest. They didn't get anywhere, so they took him to Caiaphas, the official high priest. Finally they asked him directly if he was the Messiah. Jesus said, "yes." That was all they needed to hear. They considered his answer blasphemy, the worst crime a Jew could commit. The penalty for blasphemy was death. The next morning they would hold another "official" trial and pronounce the judgment. For now they were satisfied, and went home to bed. They left Jesus with some of their soldiers, who entertained themselves by hitting Jesus, blindfolding him, and making fun of him. That was just the beginning of his suffering.

We'll continue the story in the next chapter. For now it would be good for you to read the accounts of the Last Supper and the other events of that night in each of the Gospels. Keep an eye out for the different details each writer gives. Pay special attention to John's account of the Last Supper and Jesus' last talk with his Apostles. It contains some of the most beautiful passages in all Scripture. Here's where you'll find each of the accounts:

- Matthew 26.17 to the end of the chapter.
- Mark 14.12 to the end of the chapter.
- Luke 22.7 to the end of the chapter.
- John 13 — 18.27.

This will take a while, but it is worth it.

Arrested!

DID YOU KNOW?

2,000 Years of the Mass

Our Mass of today has its origins in the Last Supper meal Jesus celebrated with his Apostles. That meal has its roots in its forerunner, the Passover meal, which the Jewish people celebrated each year from the time of Moses. Devout Jews still celebrate this Passover meal each year. It's called the Seder.

But the Mass as we have it today went through long centuries of development. Certain core parts have always been present: readings from Scripture, the words of consecration, and the offering of the consecrated bread and wine to the Father, a communion or sharing of the bread and the cup of the Lord. Those are what we might call the essentials of any Mass.

But over the centuries the Church has celebrated this meal-sacrifice in many different ways when it comes to the variables. These include things like the language used (for a long time Latin was the only official language, even though people no longer understood it), the kinds of vestments the priest is expected to wear, various prayers and hymns that are used, the gestures and symbols used — like the kiss of peace, candles, and incense.

These external differences usually came from the customs of the time, which people felt were in good taste. For example, for a long time women were expected to wear hats or veils to Mass. There was even a time when the organ was outlawed for church use because it was considered an instrument of popular music and thus unsuitable for sacred music. Today some people feel that way about guitars and other musical instruments and only want the organ. Times change!

But the core of the Mass always remains the same. Jesus becomes present under the appearances of bread and wine and he offers himself to the Father in sacrifice, re-presenting his sacrifice of Good Friday. Then we eat together, we share the Body and Blood of Christ. In doing this we become united with Jesus, his Father, and with one another. So, in a real sense, the Mass has never changed since Jesus first celebrated it on Holy Thursday evening.

What Has This Got to Do With Me?

How important is the Mass to you?

Have you any opportunities to serve others? Do you?

How do you handle tough decisions? Do you ever pray over them?

Review Questions and Activities

1. Why was the Passover so important to the Jews?
2. What important lesson did Jesus teach by washing the Apostles' feet?
3. How did Jesus feel about what he knew was going to happen to him once he was arrested?
4. Who followed Jesus to the house of Annas?
5. What crime was Jesus found guilty of by the Jewish leaders?

Scripture Focus

- *Luke 22.19-20*

Then, taking bread and giving thanks, he broke it and gave it to them, saying: "This is my body to be given for you. Do this as a remembrance of me." He did the same with the cup after eating, saying as he did so: "This cup is the new covenant in my blood, which will be shed for you."

Good Friday

When they had finished mocking him, they stripped him of the purple, dressed him in his own clothes, and led him out to crucify him.

(Mark 15.20)

We're going to ask you to read the Gospel accounts of Jesus' Passion so you can get the full story. Here it will be enough to mention some of the key events.

Crucified

Early in the morning the Jewish leaders took Jesus to Pilate. Only the Roman ruler could order Jesus' execution. From the start Pilate could see Jesus was innocent and tried to get out of having to condemn him. That's why he gave the people a choice between Jesus and Barabbas. He was sure they'd never choose Barabbas, a regular

cutthroat. Finally, Pilate gave in and had Jesus scourged. He thought once the people saw the beating Jesus received, they'd feel sorry for him. They didn't. So Pilate ordered his crucifixion. He was afraid the Jewish leaders would complain about him to the Roman emperor.

Jesus was led to Golgotha (the Skull), carrying his cross. He needed help because he was already so weakened from the scourging, lack of sleep, and lack of food.

About noon they nailed him to the cross. He hung there for three hours before he died. Soldiers kept guard and gambled for his few clothes — all the property he owned!

After he died, some friends got permission to bury him in a nearby tomb. Jewish leaders arranged to have the tomb sealed with a huge rock and posted a guard. No one could come to take his body and then claim he rose from death.

Crucifixion

Those were the bare facts. But here are a few more details to help you understand what really happened. First there is scourging. It was a standard Roman punishment for criminals. They'd use a special whip with pieces of bone or glass tied to the tips. Usually the judge would set an exact number of lashes. While Jewish law prescribed a maximum of forty, Roman law set no limit. For one condemned like Jesus, there was no limit. The soldiers assigned to give the scourging could go on as long as they wanted. Often the criminal would never survive the scourging to be crucified. Jesus did survive, but if we accept the Shroud of Turin as evidence, he had cuts all over his body by the time the soldiers quit. The crown of thorns, the mocking, the face slapping and spitting that followed weren't typical. But the soldiers were free to do whatever they wanted.

Most scholars agree that Jesus didn't carry a whole cross as pictures usually show. The upright portion was kept in place on the execution grounds. The condemned person carried the cross beam. It was maybe the size of a railroad tie. When they reached the place for the execution the prisoner's arms were attached to the cross beam. Then they raised him up, fixed the beam on the top of the pole and fastened his feet to the bottom.

They didn't always nail a criminal to the cross. Sometimes they would just tie him there. Such people could hang there for several days before they died. If they did nail a person to the cross they would drive the nails through the wrists, not the palms. Sometimes the upright portion of the cross would have a board sticking out, a kind of seat the criminal would straddle. It helped support the weight of the body. It also kept the prisoner alive longer so he could suffer more. Crucifixion was designed to cause the maximum

amount of pain for the longest time. Crucifixions usually were public events and took place where the most people could see the condemned person. Golgotha (or Calvary) was along a main road into Jerusalem and would be crowded with pilgrims that time of year. The Romans did this as a warning to others not to try anything. Usually they attached a little sign saying why the person was crucified. For example, John, a murderer, or James, a revolutionary. Jesus' crime — King of the Jews!

Why?

One question we have to ask is this: how could the people turn on Jesus? This is something of a mystery, but we should remember a few things. Jerusalem was filled with strangers, there for the feast. As devout Jews they would want to protect their religion from false prophets. They didn't know Jesus, since they were from out of the country. They would very likely be influenced by what the Jewish leaders said. Also, there are always people who for some strange reason enjoy seeing others suffer. Even today we have people who will gather and encourage some poor, confused soul on a window ledge to jump. Also keep in mind that this was the big day for the powers of evil. Evil, Satan, is real and people can do horrible things when they are under its control. Finally the Gospel tells us this was a mob. A mob isn't the same as a crowd or a gathering. A mob doesn't think. It acts on impulse. A mob is irrational.

More Than Suffering

There's one more thing to keep in mind as you read the Gospels. Too often so much is made of Jesus' suffering that we miss the real point of his execution. It's true that he suffered the most terrible kind of death. The physical pain was real and indescribable. He also suffered spiritually — mockery, betrayal, abandonment by friends, rejection by those he tried to help.

But we need to remember what that suffering really means. Jesus was trying to tell us how much he loves us. "No greater love does a man have than to lay down his life for a friend." Jesus literally sacrificed his own life so we could be freed from the powers of evil. How Jesus died isn't so important as the fact that he was willing to die for us. How he died just helps us realize how greatly he loved us.

Michelangelo's Pietà.

The Answer is YES

Also Jesus died the way he did because it was the Father's will. Jesus' death is the perfect act of obedience to God. From the beginning, people rebelled against God, seeking their own way rather than doing what God asked of them. Jesus' obedience unto death, "even death on the cross" (Philippians 2. 8), was a resounding "yes" to God, making it possible for every person to say "yes" too. Jesus' "yes" reversed human history.

The point is this. Jesus teaches us that the two most important things we can do are to love one another and obey Yahweh, our loving Father. Doing so will sometimes mean suffering. God doesn't judge us by how much we suffer. He doesn't even want us to suffer! He judges us by how much we love and by the way we say "yes" to his loving rule.

Jesus' Passion shows the way, and teaches us how to do both. When Jesus asks us, his followers, to "take up your cross and follow me" he's asking us to love each other and say "yes" to our Father. He's asking us to deny our selfish urges and desires. Often, that is painful.

The focus is really on how much Jesus loves and how perfectly he obeys his Father. Accepting torture and death is a sign of how boundless that love is. That's the message of Good Friday.

Now read these passages: Matthew 27 Mark 15; Luke 23 and John 18.28 - 19.42. Be sure to note the details.

What Has This Got to Do With Me?

Have you ever been asked to suffer for your religion? Would you be willing to?

Do you ever pray the Stations of the Cross?

Do you sometimes find it difficult to say "yes" to God? When?

Review Questions and Activities

1. Why did the Jewish leaders turn Jesus over to Pilate?
2. Why did Pilate finally order Jesus' execution?
3. What was written on the sign they hung above Jesus' cross?
4. What was more important for our salvation than the physical sufferings Jesus endured?
5. What does it mean for us to take up our cross?

Scripture Focus

- *Mark 15.20*

This is the wood of the cross. Come, let us worship.

DID YOU KNOW?

Way of the Cross

The Way of the Cross began in early times when Holy Land pilgrims would visit the actual scenes of Christ's Passion. But the stations as we know them today began to evolve as a result of strong devotion to the Passion in the twelfth and thirteenth centuries. The Franciscans did the most to promote the devotion in order to help the faithful learn about and pray over the events of Jesus' Passion. There are fourteen Stations of the Cross in all. Ten are based on the Gospel accounts. The three that describe Jesus falling on the journey to Golgotha (the third, seventh, and ninth), and the one describing Veronica wiping Jesus' face with a cloth (the sixth), are not found in the Gospel accounts but are part of our tradition.

At first, the Franciscans would erect paintings or simple statues, which described each of the fourteen events, outside along some road or trail. People would walk from one to the next, stopping at each to pray and to think about Jesus' sufferings. The devotion became popular. It was simple, but powerful. It had some movement and variety which helped people pray better. You didn't have to be educated to appreciate the story the stations told or the meaning behind the events.

Because they did become popular they were soon put up along the walls inside the churches. This devotion has remained popular right up to today, especially during Lent when we prepare to celebrate the resurrection by focusing on Jesus' sufferings and his death. We find them in almost every church and in many places we still find them outside too. Because of the work of the Franciscans to promote this devotion, the Church has given them the right to be the official installers of the Stations of the Cross when they are put up for the first time in a new church or shrine.

There are no official prayers that must be used in praying the stations. Some prefer to make up their own prayers if they are praying the stations alone. Because the stations are so simple and so powerful, and because they help us grow in understanding and appreciating what Jesus has done for us, it is one devotion that you ought to do — often.

He Is Risen

"Do not be frightened. I know you are looking for Jesus the crucified, but he is not here. He has been raised, exactly as he promised. Come and see the place where he was laid. Then go quickly and tell his disciples."

(Matthew 28.5-7)

After the Excitement

Way back in the second chapter we talked about the events surrounding Jesus' resurrection. After the surprise and excitement of those first days, things settled down a little. Peter and some of the other Apostles even returned to fishing, probably because they had to make a living somehow. People weren't supporting them the way they used to when Jesus was with them. Jesus kept showing up, usually without any warning. He wanted to keep reassuring his followers that he really was risen.

The Service of Light beginning the Easter Vigil celebration.

But, as he had warned them at the Last Supper, he would soon have to leave them. As long as Jesus was on earth with them they would depend too much on him. Once Jesus returned to his Father, the Apostles could get about their mission of proclaiming the Risen Jesus and the kingdom.

So a short time after Easter — the Gospel writers tell us forty days — Jesus was taken up into heaven. We celebrate it today as the feast of the Ascension. Before he left them, though, he told them to go to Jersusalem and wait for the gift of the Spirit. He also gave them this command:

> *". . . Go, therefore, and make*
> *disciples of all the nations.*
> *Baptize them in the name*
> *of the Father,*
> *and of the Son,*
> *and of the Holy Spirit.*
> *Teach them to carry out everything*
> *I have commanded you.*
> *And know that I am with you*
> *always, until the end of the*
> *world!"*
>
> *(Matthew 28.19-20)*

Finishing School

During those days after the resurrection and before his ascension Jesus did more than reassure the Apostles that he was risen from the dead. He put the finishing touches on their training. He reaffirmed Peter's role as head of the Apostles and of the Church (John 21.15-18). He shared with them his power to forgive sins (John 20.22-23). As we just read, he instructed them to baptize in his name. In short, Jesus completed the foundations of his Church. That Church would be born a few days after his ascension when Jesus shared his final gift — the Holy Spirit. That's what Pentecost is all about.

Pentecost

The word, Pentecost, means fifty days. The Israelites celebrated a harvest feast fifty days after the Passover feast. In Acts, Luke describes that as the day Jesus sent the Holy Spirit upon the Apostles. Today we celebrate Pentecost on the seventh Sunday after Easter, or the fiftieth day after Easter.

The coming of the Spirit is described in typical biblical terms. "Suddenly from up in the sky there came a noise like a strong, driving wind . . . . Tongues as of fire appeared, which parted and came to rest on each of them" (Acts 2.2-3). Wind and fire are often used to reveal God's presence and power. We know that the Apostles and other disciples gathered there were filled with the Holy Spirit. This marked the completion of Jesus' ministry and the beginning of the Church. Empowered by the Holy Spirit, they could now go out and, in Jesus' name, carry on Jesus' ministry to every part of the world. Their identification with Jesus was complete. Now they were truly his disciples.

The Rest of the Story

The rest of the Acts of the Apostles really tells the story of how the Spirit guided and aided the Apostles in carrying out their mission. It is sometimes called the Gospel of the Holy Spirit. In those first days Jesus' disciples really faced an impossible task. They had no authority, no education, no wealth or social influence.

That they even had the courage to try to preach is proof that they possessed the Holy Spirit. That they could preach so powerfully — and sometimes in languages they didn't even understand — is also proof. That people listened and believed is perhaps the greatest proof that Jesus had gifted his newborn Church with the Spirit so it could carry out its mission.

In His Name

The Apostles also found they could perform miracles in Jesus' name through the power of the Spirit. This too helped them in their mission. But we shouldn't get too distracted by all the glamorous side effects of the Spirit's power — like speaking in tongues or working miracles. The really important gifts of the Spirit are internal: things like courage, wisdom, understanding, love, joy, and self-control. We saw how Jesus was changed through his resurrection. In much the same way, the Apostles and other disciples were changed when Jesus shared the fullness of his Spirit with them. They were literally new men and women.

The Holy Spirit helped the first Christians in very dramatic ways so they could carry out their mission. Once the Church became firmly established this dramatic kind of help — miracles and such — became more rare. Day-to-day example is enough to proclaim the kingdom and call people to faith. By the death of the last Apostle the more direct help by the Spirit became rather rare. It still happened — and it still happens today — but now the Spirit focuses much more on helping us to be courageous, loving, generous. He helps us understand what the Scriptures contain and what God wants us to do.

We Are Gifted

There's an important message here. Through our baptism and, in a special way, through our confirmation, Jesus shares the fullness of his Spirit with us — the same Spirit the Apostles received on Pentecost. Our baptism and confirmation not only make us full members of the Church, they make us disciples, witnesses, and missionaries, just like the first Apostles.

As witnesses, we are gifted. As originally promised in Isaiah 11.1-3, we are filled with the gifts of the Holy Spirit:

- *Wisdom* — to help us know God as the highest good.

- *Understanding* — to help us know truth from lies.
- *Counsel* — to help us guide others to Jesus.
- *Fortitude* — to help us remain strong during times of crisis.
- *Knowledge* — to help us learn all that our faith calls us to believe.
- *Piety* — to help us to act always out of love of God.
- *Fear of the Lord* — to help us respect the power of God.

Being a witness to the faith may sound a little unreal to you just now. The first Apostles didn't know what they were getting into either when they first started following Jesus. At your age you too are just beginning to follow Jesus. Who knows what the Spirit will do for you if you remain a faithful follower? Remember how we said the Apostles had all kinds of weaknesses and flaws. Yet look how the Spirit transformed them. Who's to say the Spirit can't do the same for you? All you really need to do right now is to try to follow Jesus as closely as you can, the way the Apostles did. The Spirit you have received will do the rest — if you let him.

 The dove: symbol of the Holy Spirit.

DID YOU KNOW?

Seasons and Feasts

The Church year or liturgical year has four seasons to it, but they don't follow exactly the four seasons of spring, summer, fall, and winter. The Church year begins with the season of *Advent*, the four weeks we use to prepare for Christmas and the "coming of Christ." During Advent we also prepare to celebrate his Second Coming at the end of the world. Finally we prepare to celebrate Jesus' entrance into our own lives in a new, more perfect way at this point in our lives. Then comes the actual *Christmas* season when we celebrate Jesus' coming. The next season of the Church year is *Lent*. This is a forty-day time of penance and conversion in preparation for Easter, when Jesus rose from the dead and we seek to rise to new life in him. Then comes the *Easter* season itself, the most important and most joyous of the entire year. It begins with the Easter Vigil on Holy Saturday night and ends with Pentecost.

In between each of these seasons there are some weeks which we call Ordinary Time. In a sense, it is a time to catch our breath and to bring Jesus' message into our "ordinary" daily lives.

It might be worth noting that in the mind of the Church, Easter, not Christmas, is the most important feast in the Church year. Christmas announces the beginning of your salvation in Jesus. Easter celebrates salvation itself.

Besides these four seasons, which help us to go through the "history of our salvation" each year, the Church celebrates certain feasts of Mary because of her special role in the history of our salvation. We studied these in Chapter 15.

Then we have feast days for many of the saints who have enriched the Church through the centuries. Some saints are more popular with certain peoples or in certain countries, so those people celebrate these in a bigger way than others. For example, St. Patrick is special to the Irish. The feast of St. Catherine of Siena is a big day for the people of Siena in Italy. The first American-born saint is St. Elizabeth Seton, canonized in 1975. Her feast day is January 4. The Church year with its seasons and feasts is anything but dull. The Church wants us to remember, to grow — and to celebrate our salvation!

What Has This Got to Do With Me?

In what special ways do you celebrate Easter? Do you seek out the meaning of the Easter-time celebrations?

Do you feel you can be a proclaimer of the kingdom? Should you be?

Does Jesus' Spirit ever influence you? Do you let it?

Review Questions and Activities

1. What did Jesus do after his resurrection before he was taken up to heaven?
2. What do we call the feast celebrating Jesus being taken to heaven? When do we celebrate it?
3. What happened on Pentecost?
4. How did the reception of the Spirit affect the Apostles?
5. When do we receive the Spirit in a special way?

Scripture Focus

- *Matthew 28.5-6*

Unit Review

1. Why did so many people stop following Jesus?
2. Why did Jesus choose the Passover as the time to confront the Jewish leaders?
3. What was the real reason Jesus was so angry at the Jewish leaders?
4. What important lesson did Jesus teach by washing the Apostles' feet?
5. What was more important for our salvation than Jesus' physical sufferings?
6. What happened on Pentecost?

Some Words to Know

ALMS • Donations given to the poor.

ASCENSION • Jesus' departure from this earth to live forever with the Father.

BLASPHEMY • Irreverent words or actions dishonoring God.

CALVARY • The place where Jesus was crucified (also called Golgotha).

CONFIRMATION • The sacrament that completes the baptismal initiation into the Christian community by the action of the Holy Spirit.

EUCHARIST • The Real Presence of Jesus under the forms of bread and wine.

GALILEAN MINISTRY • Jesus' work during most of his public life took place in the territory of Galilee.

GOLGOTHA • The name of the place where Christ was crucified, also called Mount Calvary.

HYPOCRITE • One who pretends to be holy or virtuous.

JERUSALEM MINISTRY • Jesus' last couple of weeks were spent working and teaching around the city of Jerusalem.

PENTECOST • A feast on the seventh Sunday after Easter, commemorating the descent of the Holy Spirit on the Apostles.

SACRAMENTAL • An object that is blessed by the Church and has some special religious meaning, or acts as a reminder of some religious truth.

TITHING • The practice of giving one tenth of one's wealth to the support of the Church and care of the poor.

UNIT 5

Beyond Pentecost

INTRODUCTION

In this unit we'll see how the followers of Jesus — the Church — grew in response to their Pentecost experience. We'll see that they still had much to learn about Jesus and his teaching in those days. We'll see how that understanding continues to grow. And as we described in the first unit, we'll see how the Gospels grew during that time.

Finally, we'll see how the Church continues Jesus' mission and ministry right up to today, and how Jesus continues to be present in and through the Church.

So Jesus' story, his mission, and his ministry never end. But the story of your mission and ministry is just beginning.

The Preaching of Peter

Grow rather in grace, and in the knowledge of our Lord and Savior Jesus Christ. Glory be to him now and to the day of eternity! Amen.
(2 Peter 3.18)

For almost two thousand years before the time of Jesus there was one central truth in the Jewish religion: There is only one God, Yahweh! The worst thing Jews could do was to worship false gods. So for the followers of Jesus to grasp the idea that Jesus was himself God, the Son of the Father, was not an easy task. They did this gradually during that first century after Jesus' death and resurrection. We can even see this development in the New Testament writings. It wasn't until the fourth century, at the Council of Nicea in 325, that the young Church actually made a formal definition regarding Jesus' divinity.

Messiah and Savior

When Peter first began to preach his message he focused on two things: Jesus is Yahweh's promised Messiah; Jesus is Savior, the one sent by Yahweh to save Israel from its sins and restore it to friendship with God. Only gradually did Peter himself fully grasp Jesus' relationship to Yahweh as Yahweh's divine Son.

Jews First

Also, in the beginning, Peter didn't fully understand that the Old Covenant with its Temple, its sacrifices, and laws was totally replaced by the New Covenant established by Jesus' death and resurrection. Even after Pentecost, when he and the other Apostles went out to preach the Good News about Jesus being the Messiah, they still continued to go to the Temple and to follow the basic laws of the Old Covenant (Acts 3.1). It seems that Peter expected that first the Jews would come to believe that Jesus was the Messiah. Then the Jews, in turn, would go out and convert the Gentiles not only to belief in Jesus, but also to belief in Judaism. For example, in the beginning, when Gentiles sought baptism and membership in the community of Jesus, Peter insisted that they first be circumcised, that is, become Jews.

It was Paul, whom we'll talk about in the next chapter, who challenged this idea. This caused one of the first big controversies in the young Church. The problem was finally decided at what we now call the First Council of Jerusalem (Acts 15). Before that council Peter had a special religious experience that helped him deal with this problem. Read about it in Acts 10. From then on Peter began to understand that the Gospel should be proclaimed to Jews and Gentiles alike and that the Laws of the Old Covenant were no longer binding. That's basically what was decided at the Council of Jerusalem.

A statue of St. Peter found in St. Peter's Basilica in Rome.

A New Covenant

But for Jewish Christians, that is, Jews who accepted Jesus as Messiah, the final break with the Old Covenant did not really come until the destruction of Jerusalem and the Temple in A.D. 70. While our present-day Christianity has its roots in the Old Covenant — and much of what that Covenant teaches is included in Christian teaching — Christianity clearly is a New Covenant. The old practice of animal sacrifice, the laws on what is clean and unclean, the practice of circumcision — all these have been replaced by New Covenant laws and practices taught by Jesus and developed by the Church.

So it gradually became clear to the early Church that Jesus was not just the Jewish Messiah but the Savior of all humanity. Salvation comes from belief in him, not from following Jewish laws. Jesus became the "new Moses." This is a key theme throughout the Gospel of Matthew.

Peter himself eventually left Jerusalem. Jewish persecutions grew worse. It was now obvious that there wouldn't be the total conversion and reform of the Jewish people he had expected. He made his way to Rome where he spent his remaining years preaching Jesus to Jew and Gentile alike and in guiding the young Church.

Pope Peter I

Jesus had made it clear that Peter would be the leader of the Apostles. Even though others sometimes disagreed with Peter, as Paul did, no one questioned his role as head of the Christian community.

So when he was crucified in Rome near Vatican Hill in A.D. 64, the person chosen by the community to be his successor was then considered the head of the Church. His name was Linus, our second pope, as we now call the successors of Peter in Rome. As we know, the Vatican (where Peter is still buried) has become the headquarters of the Church throughout the world. We call it the *Roman* Catholic Church because its headquarters and the place where the successor of Peter lives are still in Rome.

The main point in all of this is that the early Christians, including the Apostles, only gradually came to a full understanding of who Jesus really was and what was really involved in believing in Jesus. At first they understood Jesus as their Messiah and Savior. Through the guidance of the Spirit they gradually came to realize that Jesus is also the divine, eternal Son of the Father.

Paul will have much to do in helping the early Church understand this. We'll see that next.

What Has This Got to Do With Me?

Does today's pope play any role in your own life?

Do you see your parish church as a house of God?

What is your attitude toward Jews?

Review Questions and Activities

1. Why did the first Christians have difficulty understanding Jesus' divinity?
2. How did Peter first think the news of salvation would spread?
3. How were the first Gentile converts treated?
4. Who challenged that idea?
5. What event helped the early Christians realize that the Old Covenant had been replaced by the New Covenant?

Scripture Focus

- *2 Peter 3.18*

DID YOU KNOW?

The Vatican

Tradition tells us Peter was martyred in Rome and buried on Vatican Hill, the site of an ancient pagan cemetery. Following that tradition, the Emperor Constantine, the first Roman Emperor to become a Christian (and also to make Christianity the official religion of the empire), ordered a church built there. It was completed and dedicated in A.D. 326 by St. Sylvester, the pope at that time.

Over the centuries that church was damaged, repaired, added to, and again damaged. Finally, in 1506, Pope Julius II decided to build a new church, one truly worthy of being St. Peter's Church. The basic plan was drawn up by Donato Bramante. Many others had a part from time to time in adding to the basic design and decoration. These included Michelangelo. No wonder it took over one hundred and fifty years to complete.

Today it is certainly the most

One view of St. Peter's Basilica in modern Rome.

famous and probably the most beautiful church in the world. It is also the largest. When crowds really get large, in the neighborhood of 100,000 or so, the people gather in the square in front of the basilica for the many celebrations and other important events held there. There aren't too many sports stadiums that can hold more than that at one time. And they were designed to hold crowds. St. Peter's was designed to hold worshipers.

Once the Vatican Hill became the seat ("see" is another word for seat) of the Church's operations, many buildings were constructed there over the years. Gradually all these buildings became a city inside the city of Rome. We call it Vatican City. The Pope's house is there (actually an apartment of rooms inside a huge building called the Apostolic Palace.)

So is the Vatican Museum, containing some of the most important works of art humans ever created. There's the Vatican Library with some of the most important and rare books ever created. There are gardens, a post office, a newspaper, even a radio station, and a tiny jail.

With the vast artistic heritage of the Vatican, some people, of course, have criticized the Church for being too concerned with wealth, but these treasures are open to the public to enjoy. That's something that would never be if they had been sold to private collectors, for instance.

So, in their own way, the art and culture of the Vatican honor Jesus, the carpenter's son from Nazareth, and an uneducated fisherman he chose to take his place in proclaiming the kingdom of God. The bottom line is simply that Peter's Church and Vatican City were built by faith and are rooted in faith. They are a monument to two thousand years of belief that Jesus is Messiah and Savior, God and man.

The Preaching of Paul

Last of all he was seen by me, as one born out of the normal course. I am the least of the apostles; in fact, because I persecuted the church of God, I do not even deserve the name. But by God's favor I am what I am.

(1 Corinthians 15.8-10)

Despite what Paul says about himself being the least of the Apostles, he ranks right next to Peter as leader and guide of the early Church. And he remains so even to this day. But it is true that he was a kind of Johnny-come-lately. He was from Tarsus, not Jerusalem. Though a Jew by blood, he was also a Roman citizen. He was a member of the Pharisee sect and had been well trained in the Jewish Law. As a dedicated Pharisee he tried to follow the Law to the letter.

It's also true that he began to persecute Jews who had converted to Jesus. In Acts we find him participating in the stoning of Stephen, the deacon (Acts 7.54-60). He was well known and feared by the early Christians because he was so energetic in seeking them out and having them arrested.

A Conversion That Really Was

In fact he was on his way to Damascus for that very purpose when Jesus appeared to him. It changed his whole life — and that of the Church. You can read about it in Acts 9.1-30. We don't know in what way Jesus revealed himself and what he taught Paul, but from that time on Paul was one of the most courageous and zealous preachers of the Gospel the Church has ever had.

Even he could rightfully boast about that fact. Here's what he says in his own defense about being specifically chosen by Christ to be an Apostle:

Are they ministers of Christ? . . . I am more: with my many more labors and imprisonments, with far worse beatings and frequent brushes with death. Five times at the hands of the Jews I received forty lashes less one; three times I was beaten with rods; I was stoned once, shipwrecked three times; I passed a day and night on the sea. I traveled continually, endangered by floods, robbers, my own people, the

Gentiles; imperiled in the city, in the desert, at sea, by false brothers; enduring labor, hardship, many sleepless nights; in hunger and thirst and frequent fastings; in cold and nakedness.

(2 Corinthians 11.23-27)

Those aren't the experiences of some armchair Christian! Once Paul saw the light, he put his whole life into proclaiming Jesus to anyone who would listen. He founded churches or Christian communities throughout the Roman Empire. Finally he was imprisoned and, tradition tell us, beheaded by the Romans at Rome in A.D. 67 or maybe earlier.

Paul, the Theologian

While Paul is rightly famous for all his missionary work, he has been of even greater service to the Church as a theologian.

Paul was the first to begin to grasp, and then find a way to explain, that Jesus was not only the Messiah and Savior, but the pre-existing, divine Son of Yahweh. He was the first to begin to grasp, and find a way to explain, that God's plan for the world, from the moment of creation, centered on Jesus. He came to understand that Jesus is not just the Messiah to the Hebrews but the very Head of all creation, through whom God made all things and by whom all things would be saved and restored to the Father as a new creation. This is very deep. After all we are at the heart of mystery. Even Peter once wrote that Paul's teaching can be hard to understand. Peter never challenged it; he just said it was deep (2 Peter 3.15-16).

Son of God

Here is just one sample of what Paul teaches about Jesus:

He (Jesus) is the image of the invisible God, the first-born of all creatures. In him everything in heaven and on earth was created,

things visible and invisible, whether thrones or dominations, principalities or powers; all were created through him and for him. He is before all else that is. In him everything continues in being. It is he who is head of the body, the church; he who is the beginning, the first-born of the dead, so that primacy may be his in everything. It has pleased God to make absolute fullness reside in him, and by means of him, to reconcile everything in his person, both on earth and in the heavens, making peace through the blood of his cross.

(*Colossians 1.15-20*)

To understand Jesus in such a way is a big jump from when the Apostles first followed the carpenter's son from Nazareth and wondered whether or not he was a prophet. That kind of growth in understanding by Paul and by the early Church could only be the work of the Holy Spirit. The Spirit never stopped working to enlighten and inspire the Church from that first Pentecost. The effects were becoming obvious.

A Library of Christianity

We find all these teachings about Jesus in Paul's epistles. They contain more than deep theology. They also contain many practical suggestions and instructions in Christian living. These letters were written to the churches he had founded, and some of what they contain deal only with local matters — like correcting abuses and divisions and petty jealousies. But the letters were gradually collected and shared with all the churches. That's why they finally found their way into the official New Testament. Even today we rely on Paul's teaching to help us understand Jesus, the Church — and ourselves. You will eventually want to read them all, many times.

A Human Saint

For all of Paul's great missionary work and for all his great theological teaching, he was still human. He had his weaknesses which he had to struggle against. In one letter he even said of himself:

. . . I was given a thorn in the flesh, an angel of Satan to beat me and keep me from getting proud. Three times I begged the Lord that this might leave me. He said to me, "My grace is enough for you, for in weakness power reaches perfection." And so I willingly boast of my weakness instead, that the power of Christ may rest upon me.

(*2 Corinthians 12.7-9*)

Many people have tried to guess what Paul's "thorn in the flesh" was. Suggestions have ranged from epilepsy to temptations against purity to

THE LETTERS OF ST. PAUL

Letter and date	Doctrinal Teaching	Moral Teaching
1 Thessalonians A.D. 49-51	Destiny of the dead; Christ's Second Coming	Love one another; right sexual conduct; live peaceably; patience in persecution, no revenge
2 Thessalonians A.D. 49-51	Purpose of suffering; Final Judgment; Second Coming	Persevere in the faith; pray for the Gospel's success; avoid idleness; do what is right
Galatians A.D. 54	Faith in Christ supersedes the Law of Moses	We are sons of God; obey Christ in faith; reject all self-indulgent passions, desires. Do good while you can
1 Corinthians A.D. 56	We are part of Christ's Body; resurrection of the body; one master, Christ; one message, Cross; God will never try you beyond your strength; unity among local churches everywhere; true meaning of love	Avoid Christians who lead immoral lives; reject fornication; avoid scandal; mutual self-giving in marriage is the rule; divorce is forbidden; reverent awareness of the Body and Blood of the Lord in the Eucharist
2 Corinthians A.D. 57	Each person will receive what he deserves from God, for the good or evil he did; we are temples of the living God	Be servants of God by purity, knowledge, patience, kindness, holiness and love; share with the poor; be generous; do what is right
Romans A.D. 57	Existence of God is humanly knowable; salvation through faith in Christ; eternal life is our destiny	Behave according to God's ways not the world's; show charity to all, including enemies; obey civil authorities
Philippians	Divine pre-existence of Jesus	Be perfect children of God; seek to know Christ
Colossians A.D. 62-62	Divine pre-existence of Jesus; Christ is master of the universe	Reject fornication, impurity, guilty passion, greed, evil desires, anger, dirty talk, spitefulness
Ephesians A.D. 61-63	Unity in Christ; one Lord, one faith, one baptism; we are members of the Body of Christ	Grow into Christ; reject an aimless life; speak the truth, help others, do not steal, do good, do not sadden the Holy Spirit, hold no grudges or spite

alcoholism. No one knows for sure. But we do know this: even the greatest people in the Church will suffer from weaknesses and must depend on Jesus' power, not their own, in order to remain faithful. So we should never let our own weaknesses get us down. Instead we need to continue to trust in Jesus' power and his love for us.

What Has This Got to Do With Me?

Do you trust that Jesus can help you with your weaknesses?

Have you ever thought of being a missionary?

How real is Jesus for you?

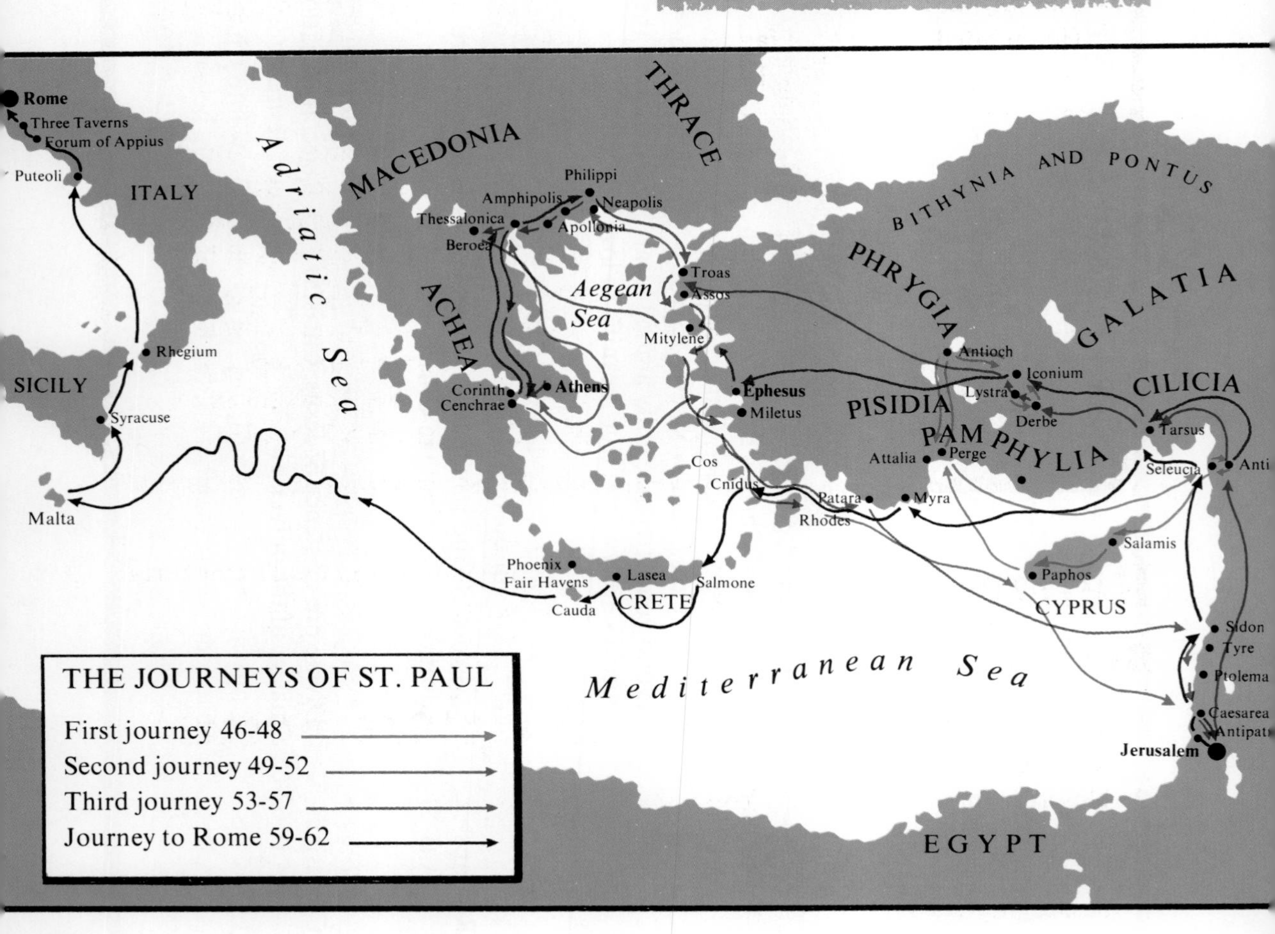

DID YOU KNOW?

St. Paul's Journeys

Paul made three major missionary journeys. Here are some facts about them:

- First Journey: From about A.D. 44-49 (Acts 13-14).

He traveled through Asia Minor in the Provinces of Cyprus, Pamphylia, Pisidia and Lycaonia. He founded churches of faith communities in Antioch, Iconium and Derbe.

- Second Journey: From A.D. 50-53 (Acts 15-18).

On this journey he was accompanied by Silas and later joined by Timothy and Luke. First he returned to the churches in Antioch, Iconium and Derbe. Then he went to the Province of Galatia. From there he went to what was called Europe (area of Greece) where he founded churches in Philippi, Thessalonica and Corinth. He also preached in Athens. On his return to Antioch, he stopped at Ephesus, where he founded another church, and then went to Caesarea near Jerusalem.

- Third Journey: From A.D. 53-58 (Acts 18-28).

He first covered much the same region he covered in his second journey, visiting the churches he founded. He used Ephesus as his headquarters. He was making plans to travel to Spain but was arrested and imprisoned in Caesarea and eventually taken to Rome where he was beheaded.

Review Questions and Activities

1. What was Paul's early relationship to the Church?
2. Describe some of the hardships Paul suffered to preach the Gospel.
3. What did Paul do for the Church besides his missionary work?
4. Where do we find Paul's teachings?
5. What kept Paul humble?

Scripture Focus

- *1 Corinthians 15.8-10*

Matthew, Luke, and the Infancy Narratives

She gave birth to her first-born son and wrapped him in swaddling clothes and laid him in a manger, because there was no room for them in the place where travelers lodged.
(Luke 2.7)

It probably seems strange to begin talking about the birth of Jesus now that we are almost at the end of the story. But in terms of seeing how the early Church's understanding of Jesus grew, this is actually the time to see what the Gospels tell us about Jesus' birth.

The written Gospels took their final form after the Church had come to a clearer understanding of Jesus' divinity and his preexistence as Yahweh's eternal Son. Many of the epistles of Paul, for example, were circulating before the first Gospel account was written.

First Is Last

The stories of Jesus' birth contained in the Gospels of Luke and Matthew were in a sense added to the earlier form of the Gospel found in Mark. Mark makes no mention of Jesus' birth. Those stories were written for believers who had already accepted the divinity of Jesus. They were written to reinforce and enlighten that faith. Most importantly, they were written for adults.

Too often when we think of Jesus' birth we think in terms of how we celebrate Christmas today. In our society, Christmas is for children. We talk about "baby Jesus" and have images of cuddly lambs, singing angels, and toys for the little ones. Probably the Gospel writers would be confused by how we have come to treat the birth of Jesus in our time. They approached it in a different, more theological way.

Certainly there is nothing wrong with the joy and gift giving and singing that are part of Christmas celebrations. But here we want to take a closer look at what the Gospel writers were trying to tell us.

A view of Jerusalem today.

Some Comparisons

The first thing you'll notice is that the two accounts we do have (in Matthew and Luke) are quite different in many details. The main reason is that they were both writing for different audiences. Matthew was writing for Jewish converts and his goal was to strengthen their belief that Jesus fulfilled the Messianic prophecies. So he starts his Gospel by tracing Jesus' family tree back to Abraham, through King David's line. Luke, writing for Gentiles, traces Jesus' family through other lines all the way back to Adam. He wanted to show Jesus was Savior for the Gentiles as well as the Jews.

Matthew, writing for Jews familiar with the Old Testament, makes all kinds of direct and indirect references to the Hebrew Scriptures in telling his story. He quotes directly from Isaiah, Micah, and Jeremiah. He makes reference to Numbers 24.17 when he speaks of the star. He makes reference to Psalm 72.10 and Isaiah 60.6 in adding the touch about gifts of gold and frankincense. The flight into and return from Egypt are clear parallels to the Exodus story.

In other words, Matthew's story is filled with theology, theological symbols, and prophecies fulfilled. He is not telling a fairy tale.

Luke, writing for Gentiles unfamiliar with the Old Testament, does not use nearly as many Old Testament references. Instead he adds details that would appeal to Gentile believers, many of whom were probably the poor and outcasts of their society. He is proclaiming good news for the poor. He is giving a message of joy. Joy is a dominant theme in his story and throughout his Gospel. So he adds details like Mary's visitation — a time

A "Nativity" reliquary.

of joy. He makes mention of Jesus' birth in some kind of cave or stable used by animals. His crib is a manger. The first to hear the joyous news about his birth are shepherds — society's poor who can identify with stables and poverty.

But Luke doesn't talk about the visit of the Magi, the star, the Flight into Egypt or the Slaughter of the Innocents. These would not have helped his Gentile readers and didn't fit into his purpose.

What both Matthew and Luke do have in common is their insistence that Jesus was conceived by the direct influence of God. They agree that Mary was a virgin and that Jesus had no human father. Their belief in Jesus' divinity as well as his special role in history are the reason for stressing this point.

A Different Purpose

Obviously neither story is an eyewitness account, but both can certainly be trusted to be handing on to us "precisely" what the original eyewitnesses gave to them. Luke even makes that point at the beginning of his Gospel. So, we can suppose that Mary did share some of the details with the early Church before she died. Perhaps living relatives of Jesus would remember other things. There would certainly seem to be sufficient basis for including details such as being born in a cave, for example, and for the birth taking place in Bethlehem.

But much of what each story contains, especially Matthew's version, should be read primarily as a means of proclaiming the risen Lord and Savior of the world. Their purpose is to proclaim both the humanity and the divinity of Jesus. He was born of a woman like all of us and had to go through a period of growing up like all of us. But unlike us he was also God's Son sent to save us. That's what the early Church had come to understand by the time these infancy stories were included in the Gospels.

A Summary

By putting the stories together we can see the basis for most of the key images we now use in celebrating Christmas and related feasts. These include the following:

Gospel of Matthew (written for Jewish believers):
- Virgin Birth.
- Joseph's dreams.
- The Magi and the star; no mention is made of camels, but that was a normal way for people from the East to travel.
- Gold, frankincense, and myrrh — gift giving.
- Herod and his plot to kill Jesus.
- The flight into Egypt.
- The Feast of the Holy Innocents.

Gospel of Luke (written for Gentile believers):
- The Annunciation.
- The Visitation.
- The stable, manger; filled inn; swaddling clothes; the shepherds and angels. Animals like the donkey, sheep and cows or oxen aren't mentioned but they could be found around a stable; a donkey was used by poor people for travel.
- Jesus' circumcision.

Now is a good time to read and compare the two Gospel stories.

What Has This Got to Do With Me?

Do you read the Gospels with faith?

Can you tell the Christmas story to a friend?

What elements in our present-day Christmas celebration ought to be questioned?

Review Questions and Activities

1. For whom did Matthew write?
2. For whom did Luke write?
3. What is the purpose of the infancy narratives?
4. Who includes the story of the Magi and the Flight into Egypt?
5. What does Luke include that isn't mentioned by Matthew?

Scripture Focus

- *Luke 2.7*

DID YOU KNOW?

Christmas Crèche

Tradition tells us that St. Francis was the first to set up a crèche or crib scene as a means to help the peasant people understand the Christmas story. (Crèche is a French word for crib.)

The crib scene traditionally included the people and things described in the Gospel accounts: Jesus, Mary, Joseph, the angels, shepherds, and wise men. Sheep and other animals were added. There was always a star.

Over the years the devotion caught on and now we can find a crib scene anywhere Christians celebrate Christmas. Special prayers like the blessing of the crib and other devotions have developed.

It is not unusual today to find some churches using life-size statues and even live people and real animals to reenact the scene of Jesus' birth.

Artists have used all their talent to carve statues for the scene and some are now considered priceless works of art, displayed in museums rather than churches.

This kind of devotion is good, drawing attention to the fact that Jesus was once a baby — a real person. But our faith must grow as Jesus grew. The Jesus we are called to believe in and follow is the risen Lord who calls us to adult faith and adult behavior.

CHAPTER 28

John Preaches About Jesus

In the beginning was the Word;
the Word was in God's presence,
and the Word was God.
He was present to God in the beginning.
Through him all things came into being,
and apart from him nothing came to be.
Whatever came to be in him found life,
life for the light of men.
The light shines on in darkness,
a darkness that did not overcome it. . . .

He was in the world,
and through him the world was made,
yet the world did not know who he was.
To his own he came,
yet his own did not accept him. . . .

The Word became flesh
and made his dwelling among us,
and we have seen his glory:
the glory of an only Son coming from the Father,
filled with enduring love. . . .

For while the law was given through Moses, this enduring love came through Jesus Christ. No one has ever seen God. It is God the only Son, ever at the Father's side, who has revealed him.

(John 1.1-5, 10-11, 14, 17-18)

We've Come a Long Way. . .

That's how John's Gospel, the last to be written, begins. It's obvious that by then the Church, with the guidance of the Spirit, had come to fully understand Jesus as God's divine, preexistent Son become man. "Understand" here means that they believed and knew Jesus is both God and man. It doesn't mean they really understood it in the way we can understand some scientific law, like the effect of heat and cold on water. They understood *that* Jesus is both God and man. They could not — and we still cannot fully — explain *how* it is possible. It remains a mystery.

In the Church we have a special word for this mystery of God becoming man: Incarnation. *Carnis* is the Latin word for flesh. Incarnation means that the Son of God became flesh, human, a man — just like all humans except for sin.

So John is writing for a Church that believes in this mystery of Incarnation. Jesus is the incarnation of the eternal Word of God. The introduction to the Gospel sets the tone for what is, in a real sense, a different kind of Gospel. It reflects a Church that now has a well-developed theology.

A Different Kind of Gospel

That's why John's Gospel uses so many theological symbols and images in describing Jesus. He is the Light of the world. Faith is seeing, being enlightened by this Light. Evil is described as darkness, and lack of faith as blindness, a refusal to be enlightened by the Light of the world.

Jesus is described as the Way, the Truth, and the Life. Many references are made to the new life Jesus will give: he gives us the Bread of Life, namely himself, in the Eucharist. He gives us living water, his Spirit, in the waters of our baptism. He is the Resurrection and the Life.

In other words, while John's Gospel retells the story of Jesus of Nazareth as the others do, his real focus is on the Incarnate Word, on the divinity of Jesus which is enfleshed in human nature. A good example of how different John's Gospel is from the other three is that he uses none of Jesus' parables. Instead he presents Jesus as giving a number of long speeches or

Jesus: the Way, the Truth, and the Life.

conversations. In this way the Gospel teaches us much more directly. These talks by Jesus are constructed to reveal the meaning behind Jesus' parables and other teaching and actions. Jesus is God's Word speaking to us!

These speeches and conversations contain the core teachings in John's Gospel. They include Jesus' conversation with Nicodemus (John 3), his conversation with the Samaritan woman (John 4), his argument against the Jewish leaders (John 5), his long talk on the Eucharist (John 6), his talk with the Jews after he forgave the woman taken in adultery (John 8), his Good-Shepherd speech (John 10), and his most important conversation with the Apostles during the Last Supper (John 13-17). You'll want to read all of these.

John didn't present all of Jesus' miracles either. He usually presents a miracle as a kind of occasion for one of the speeches. Of all the miracles Jesus worked, John selected only those that would best fit into the approach he developed. Also John makes no real attempt to follow any exact order of events. For example, in John's Gospel Jesus is shown cleansing the Temple at the very beginning of his public ministry. The other three have this happening only during Holy Week.

Eyewitness Theologian

For all these reasons we can see that John didn't set out to write a Gospel modeled after the ones that already existed. Those gave us a more or less complete story that followed a chronological pattern of events, even though they were written in the light of faith. John is clearly writing a "theology" of Jesus' life and is much more selective in using the actual events. John, as one of the eyewitnesses, was certainly familiar with all of Jesus' public life and knew when certain things occurred. But since he was writing a "theology" of Jesus rather than a biography, he explains the meaning of the events rather than just telling when they happened. When you read any of John's Gospel it will be helpful if you keep this in mind.

The Hardest Book Is the Last

John's Gospel was written after the Church had been in existence for about seventy years. It summarizes what the Church had come to know and believe about Jesus, the Word Incarnate. To this Gospel John added one other book, the last one in the New Testament. It is called the Book of Revelation or the Apocalypse.

Of all the books in the New Testament, this is the hardest to understand. Even today, scholars don't agree on what it all means. It's a special kind of writing. It speaks of visions of the life to come. It's filled with all kinds of imagery and symbolic words and actions.

All agree on this much. It tells us that the forces of evil will continue to fight against the Church until the end of time, but in the end Jesus will come again and the Church will be victorious.

It clearly warns about persecutions, but it is not clear whether it refers to persecutions that the Church had already experienced or persecutions yet to come.

Here's a short sample of the kind of writing you can find in the book:

I saw in heaven another sign, great and awe-inspiring; seven angels holding the seven final plagues which would bring God's wrath to a climax.

I then saw something like a sea of glass mingled with fire. On the sea of glass were standing those who had won the victory over the beast and its image, and also the number that signified its name. They were holding the harps used in worshiping God, and they sang the song of Moses, the servant of God, and the song of the Lamb.

(Revelation 15.1-3)

As you can tell, this is a very fascinating, but hard book to understand. For now, at least, you will want to focus your attention on the Gospels and Epistles. At some later time, you may want to study more about the Book of Revelation.

What Has This Got to Do With Me?

When you think of Jesus do you pay more attention to his humanity or his divinity?

How is Jesus the Way, the Truth, and the Life for you?

How is Jesus God's Word for you?

Review Questions and Activities

1. What does the Incarnation mean for Christians?
2. How does John present Jesus' teaching, as compared with the other Gospels?
3. What is John actually presenting in his Gospel?
4. What is the Apocalypse?
5. What symbols does John use to describe good and evil?

Scripture Focus

- *John 1.1*

In the beginning was the Word;
the Word was in God's presence,
and the Word was God.

DID YOU KNOW?

Three Heresies

As people struggled to understand and explain the mystery of the Incarnation, many mistaken ideas or heresies developed. Heresy comes from the Greek word meaning "to choose." A herectic — or one who followed a false idea — *chose* his own idea over the ideas or teaching held by the rest of the Christian community. Heresy is a false teaching, while a heretic is a person who chooses a false teaching.

The three biggest heresies about Jesus being God-Man are these:

- Jesus is a man adopted by God as his son and was thus made Godlike. This heresy was called Arianism after the man who first taught it. Basically it denies Jesus' divinity.

- Jesus is actually God in a human "costume." This heresy accepted Jesus' divinity but said he wasn't really a human. He only took on a human disguise. For example, he acted as he suffered on the cross but really didn't. Basically it denies Jesus' humanity and the reality of his human experience.

- Jesus is divine and also had a human body but wasn't completely human. He had a human body but didn't have a human spirit or soul. Basically this heresy taught that Jesus is fully divine and "almost human."

In answer to all these heresies or false ideas the Church always stayed with the same teaching, revealed in the Gospels. Jesus is fully human. Jesus is fully divine. That's a mystery. No human explanation is possible. But the Church knows it is true.

Today it is popular to describe Jesus as only human. Maybe the greatest man who ever lived, but only a man, like Gandhi, Mohammed, Buddha. He is a religious leader, but certainly not divine and certainly not risen from the dead. Those teachings are mistaken. They are heresies.

Note how all heresies actually try to take the easy way out by denying one half of the mystery. They focus on divinity *or* humanity. The Church has always taught that in order to understand Jesus we must keep both Jesus' divinity and his humanity together. That calls for faith.

Jesus and the Church

Live on in me, as I do in you.
No more than a branch can bear
fruit of itself
apart from the vine,
can you bear fruit
apart from me.
I am the vine, you are the branches.
(John 15.4-5)

The Apostles and early Christians firmly believed that Jesus still remained present with them even though he no longer was visible to them. He was present through the Holy Spirit which he sent them. They really were like branches drawing their life and fruitfulness from their union with Jesus. It was he who worked and taught and healed through them. Paul said it this way: "I have been crucified with Christ, and the life I live now is not my own; Christ is living in me" (Galatians 2.19-20). He also said, "Continue, therefore, to live in Christ Jesus the Lord, in the spirit in which you received him" (Colossians 2.6). That's how convinced the early Christians were that they were united to Jesus and that he remained with them.

Sacraments

This has remained true throughout the history of the Church even to this very day. Jesus remains with us; and all faithful Christians baptized into Christ's life are united with him and live in him. This doesn't mean we are going to constantly experience visions or hear voices. But through faith we *know* Jesus is with us. Besides Jesus' personal spiritual presence to all believers, Jesus is present in several special ways in his Church. The first of these is his presence through the seven sacraments, which he instituted. Each of the sacraments *make present again* (re-presents) those actions. Jesus, under the sign of each sacrament, is present, doing what the sign signifies. For example, in the sacrament of reconciliation Jesus is actually forgiving sins under the signs of confession and absolution. He is forgiving us just as he forgave so many sinners when he walked visibly on earth. In the sacrament of confirmation he is present sending the Holy Spirit to

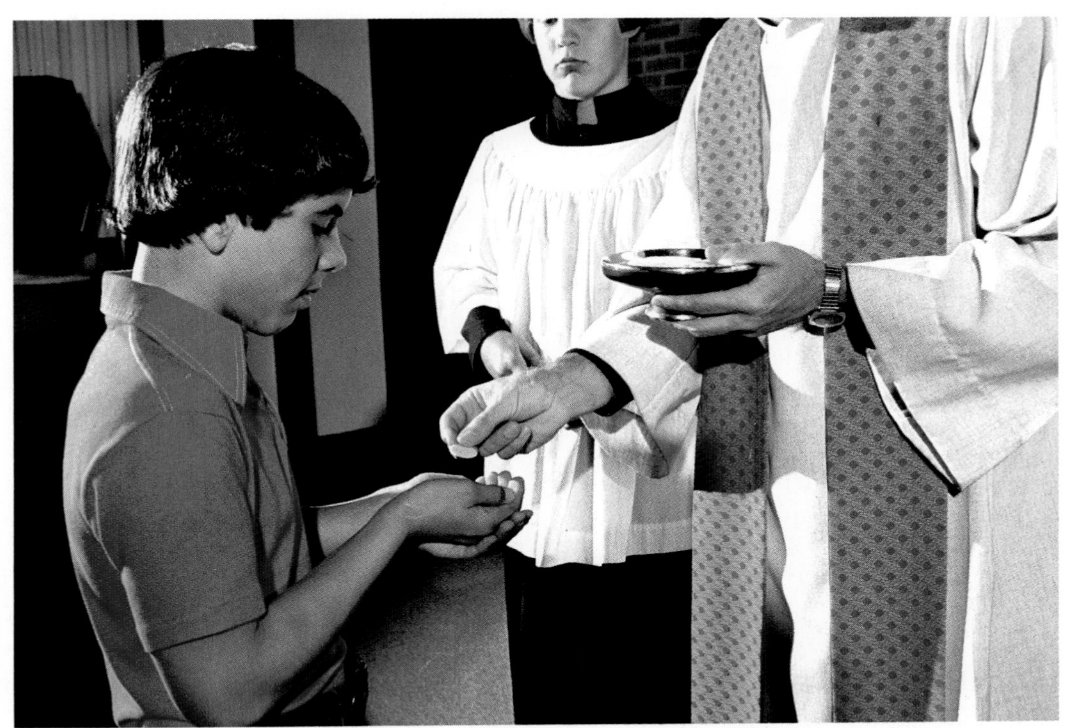

The Church considers the celebration of the Eucharist the single most important thing we can do.

us under the signs of the anointing with oil and the laying on of hands. He is present in the sacrament of the anointing of the sick, with his comfort and healing, just as he was when he walked through the towns of Galilee.

In other words, by instituting the sacraments Jesus has established a way to remain present and continue the same ministry he began two thousand years ago. Our sacraments aren't just "religious rites." They are signs of Christ's presence. But even more. They are the very actions of Christ that give us a share in the divine life and change us in various ways if our hearts are open to him.

Eucharist

This is especially true of the Eucharist, the sacrament of Christ's presence. Under the signs of bread and wine he has found a way to be united to us, *literally*. Through these same signs of bread and wine he has established a way for us to be united to one another in him. The Eucharist, instituted on Holy Thursday at the Last Supper, is unique among all the sacraments for this reason. In the other sacraments, Jesus is present under the signs to do some specific thing — forgive us, heal us, unite us in marriage, share his priestly powers. In the Eucharist Jesus is present just to be present — as God Incarnate, our Savior, our friend, our source of life. He is present not merely spiritually, but totally, Body, Blood, soul, and divinity. In fact, all the other sacraments are rooted in the Eucharist, that is, in Jesus' desire to be present to us throughout all of history. That's why the Church considers the celebration of the Eucharist the single most important thing we can do and why the Eucharist is at the very center of the Church's life.

So, the seven sacraments stand out as completely special ways for Christians to come into contact with Christ's saving work.

Community

There is a second way Jesus can be present to his faithful followers. It is rooted in his words, "Where two or three are gathered in my name, there am I in their midst" (Matthew 18.20).

The Church understands this to be a promise that anytime it gathers as Church to do the work of the Christ, he will be present too, blessing and guiding. In this sense the Church itself is a sign of Jesus' presence and action in the world. Now, that's a more general kind of presence than Christ's presence in the seven sacraments, but it does allow us to think of the Church as a sacrament too.

There are two kinds of effects when Jesus is present in the community. The first builds up the Church. That is, whenever the Church gathers to make some important decision or do something to help it do Christ's work, Jesus is there. Externally, all you can see is a group of people talking, maybe arguing. But Jesus is there too, guiding and directing. Through faith we can experience his presence in this kind of talking, working, even arguing.

The other effect of Jesus' promise to be

Where two or three are gathered in Jesus' name, he is in their midst . . . anywhere in the world.

with the community is the one it has on those outside the community. When the Church gathers for any reason, whether for prayer, to do some service, to fight some evil, we are making Jesus, his words, and his actions present in the world — literally! By these public actions of the Church, nonbelievers are given an opportunity to experience the presence and ministry of Jesus.

His Word

The third way Jesus is present to his believers is through his word. The written word of Scripture is a living word, directed to us every time it is proclaimed at Mass or read privately in our own room. The Holy Spirit inspired it when it was written down, and he likewise inspires us to understand it or at least seek to understand it better as we grow in faith and experience what Christ is saying to us today in our own lives.

And You

So Jesus is present in special ways to each person baptized into his life. Jesus is present in all the sacraments, but in a special way in the Eucharist, the root and foundation of all the others. Jesus is present within the community and he is present to the world through the community. This means *you* too can be a kind of sacrament. He is present in his word, handed down and preserved for us in the Scriptures.

Jesus be with you! The Lord be with you! That was the prayer of the early Church. It is still the prayer of the Church. And it's always answered.

What Has This Got to Do With Me?

Do you ever worship Jesus in the Blessed Sacrament?

How and when do you most experience Jesus' presence in your life?

Do you ever make Jesus present to others?

Review Questions and Activities

1. How would you define a sacrament?
2. Why is the Eucharist a special way for Jesus to be present to us?
3. Besides the sacraments, in what other ways is Jesus present to us?
4. In what way are we a sacrament?
5. What does the image of the vine and branches mean?

Scripture Focus

- *John 15.4-5*

The Blessed Sacrament

The practice of preserving some of the consecrated bread (Jesus under the sign of bread) began in the early Church. Sharing this bread at the eucharistic meal was always the highlight of the liturgy. It was a union with the Lord Jesus and a sign of the unity among the people. For this reason they'd save some of the bread for people who couldn't be present — the sick, those in prison, travelers. Some members of the community would bring the eucharistic bread to these people.

They'd keep this eucharistic bread in a special place. Because this bread is actually Jesus' Body and Blood, they considered this place sacred and eventually called it a Tabernacle — after the Old Testament Tabernacle, where Yahweh dwelt with his people, and where all the Hebrews' sacred objects were kept.

By the Middle Ages the Church kept the eucharistic bread not just for those who couldn't be present at Mass. They kept it to have Jesus with them. Devotions to the Blessed Sacrament (the words they used for the eucharistic presence of Christ) gradually became popular. These included:

- Feast of Corpus Christi (The Solemnity of the Body and Blood of Christ): This is still celebrated each spring. It usually includes a procession where the Blessed Sacrament is carried throughout the neighborhood or church and adored by the faithful.

- Benediction: In this devotion the eucharistic bread is placed in a monstrance (a sacred vessel with a special glassed-in space for the consecrated bread). The priest blesses the people with the monstrance, after certain prayers and hymns. In effect, it is Jesus under the sign of the eucharistic bread who is giving the blessing. (The word monstrance is from the Latin "to show.")

- Forty Hours Devotion: For forty hours the parish worships the Blessed Sacrament — around the clock — and ends the celebration with a procession and benediction. A variation is the Holy Hour. It is like the Forty Hours but only lasts an hour and doesn't include the procession.

Also, out of deep reverence for the Lord, the Blessed Sacrament is reserved in a side altar during the celebration of the Lord's suffering and death — from the close of the Holy Thursday celebration to the Easter Vigil Mass.

Jesus and You

"Blest are they who have not seen and have believed."
Jesus performed many other signs as well — signs not recorded here — in the presence of his disciples. But these have been recorded to help you believe that Jesus is the Messiah, the Son of God, so that through this faith you may have life in his name.

(John 20.29-31)

A Good Note

That's how John ends his Gospel. It is also a good note on which to end this course. We have seen what the Apostles have to tell us about Jesus of Nazareth. They were eyewitnesses. They came to believe he is the Son of God. They shared their story to call us to the same faith. We are asked to take their word for it, and "blest are they who have not seen and have believed" (John 20.29).

To believe doesn't mean we naively think every word in the Gospels happened exactly as it is told. Different Gospel writers give different views of the same event, explaining events in the light of faith. Yet, there should never be any doubt that the historical events themselves actually happened — from the virgin birth onwards. In the Gospels, we are not dealing with fairy tales. We are listening to the witness of the Apostles.

More Than Truth

But the faith we are called to is more than just a faith in the truth of the Gospels. We are called to faith in Jesus. To believe in Jesus is to accept him as our Savior and our God. To accept him as our Savior and our God is to entrust ourselves to him, to become disciples. To believe in Jesus is to follow him in our daily lives, not just to accept and memorize truths about him.

In other words, for believers faith isn't a "thing." It is a relationship. Ultimately, that's what the Gospels — and Jesus — call us to: a relationship with Jesus as our brother, our friend, our Savior, and our God.

The mistake the Pharisees, scribes, and other leaders made in Jesus' time was to turn religion into rules rather than into a relationship. They got so involved in explaining and following the rules of the Jewish religion that they forgot their real purpose: a means to deepen the relationship with God. Even today some people still make that mistake.

Keep It Growing

Since the faith we are called to is really a relationship with Jesus, it can keep growing in our lives. Faith is not something we get once and for all, full-blown. Faith keeps growing — or it should. We saw that in the lives of the Apostles. To say it another way, our friendship with Jesus keeps deepening, as any friendship does.

As faith grows, so does understanding. What we understand about Jesus and his teachings should also continue to grow and deepen as our relationship with Jesus grows and deepens.

A good example of this would be our approach to the Eucharist. As our friendship or faith in Jesus grows, we gain a deeper appreciation and understanding of the Eucharist and its importance. But if someone doesn't have a close faith relationship with Jesus, the Eucharist won't mean much.

The same is true of the creed. We pray together at Mass what the Church has assembled as the basic elements of our faith (Nicene Creed). But as our own faith grows, so does our understanding of these collected truths about God revealed. With greater faith, the words take on greater meaning. (See p. 193.)

So that's the call and the challenge contained in the Gospel. We are called to accept Jesus as our Savior and our God. We are called to entrust ourselves to him, to enter into a relationship with him. And we are called to continue to grow in that relationship and in our understanding of Jesus all our life. Remember, "blest are they who have not seen and have believed."

Have a good summer!

What Has This Got to Do With Me?

If Jesus were to ask you today, "Who do you say I am?" how would you answer?

Do you consider Jesus your friend?

Do you think your faith has grown this year?

Unit Review

1. Why did the first Christians have difficulty understanding Jesus' divinity?
2. What did Paul do for the Church besides his missionary work?
3. Compare the infancy narratives of Matthew and Luke.
4. What symbols does John use to describe good and evil?
5. In what ways are we a sacrament?
6. What is the call contained in the Gospels?

Scripture Focus

- *John 20.29*

DID YOU KNOW?

Official Saints

The Church has a special way of talking about people who accepted the call and the challenge to follow Jesus. It shows them special honor by calling them saints. (Anybody, however, including you, is a saint if he or she follows Jesus faithfully, even if that person doesn't get the Church's public recognition.)

The saints are grouped under these titles:

• Martyrs (means witnesses in Greek): These are disciples who were killed for believing in Jesus. They gave witness to their faith in Jesus.

• Popes, bishops, and priests: Holy people who served the Church in these official roles.

• Holy men and women: This is a general class. It used to be divided into several groups: widows, virgins, confessors. Basically it was for holy people who didn't hold any special position in the Church.

• Doctors: These are people who helped the Church in a special way by their teaching.

Sometimes a person might fit under several of these titles, so we have Church feasts for "Pope and Martyr" or "Virgin and Martyr," etc.

The bottom line is this: We have a rich history of people who followed Jesus as best they could. They are examples for us. They are our brothers and sisters. They are people we can pray to for help and people whom we should honor.

Some Words to Know

APOCALYPSE • The book of the New Testament, written by John, which describes his revelations and the future of the Church.

ARIANISM • The heresy which denies Jesus' divinity.

CHRISTMAS • The feast celebrating Jesus' birth.

COUNCIL • Meeting of leaders of the Church to decide on areas of concern for the Church.

EPISTLE • A New Testament letter or writing of instruction.

GENTILE • Anyone who was not a Jew. A non-believer.

HERESY • An idea or teaching which someone chooses contrary to the teaching of the Christian community.

INCARNATION • The mystery of Jesus, truly God, becoming man.

INFANCY NARRATIVES • The stories of Jesus' birth and the surrounding events as found in Luke and Matthew.

PERSECUTION • The harassment or killing of people because of their religious belief, ethnic origin, or social outlook. For example, many Christians were persecuted for their belief in Jesus.

RECONCILIATION • The sacrament in which Jesus heals and forgives us of our sins.

SACRAMENTS • Actions of Christ that give us a share in the divine life and change us in various ways if our hearts are open to him.

THEOLOGY • The study of God and things pertaining to God.

VATICAN • The city within the city of Rome where the pope lives and directs the affairs of the Church.

VIRGIN BIRTH • Jesus being conceived and born in a special manner, without a human father.

APPENDIX

Glossary

ADULTERY — The act of a married person having sexual relations with a person other than his or her spouse.

ALMS — Donations given to the poor.

ANNUNCIATION — The feast that celebrates the event in Mary's life when she was asked to be the mother of Jesus.

APOCALYPSE — The last book of the New Testament, written by John, which describes his revelations and the future of the Church.

APOSTLE — A special representative or messenger for Jesus.

ARIANISM — The heresy which denies Jesus' divinity.

ASCENSION — Jesus' departure from this earth to live forever with the Father.

ASSUMPTION — The feast that celebrates Mary's being taken into heaven, body and soul.

BAPTISM — Sacrament of the Church which initiates new members into the Christian community, freeing them from original sin and all sin.

BLASPHEMY — Irreverent words or actions dishonoring God.

CALVARY — The place where Jesus was crucified. See also Golgotha.

CHRIST — The Greek word for anointed one or Messiah.

CHRISTMAS — The feast celebrating Jesus' birth.

CONFIRMATION — The sacrament that completes the baptismal initiation into the Christian community by the action of the Holy Spirit.

CONTRITION — A feeling of true sorrow.

CONVERTS — Those who have changed from one religion to another.

COUNCIL — Meeting of leaders of the Church to decide on areas of concern for the Church.

COVENANT — An agreement, either between persons or between God and a person or people.

CRUCIFIXION — The manner of putting someone to death by means of nailing or binding the victim on a cross.

DISCIPLE — A student or one who follows another's preaching.

EPISTLE — A New Testament letter or writing of instruction.

ESSENES — A religious group who lived much as our monks do today, in communities apart from the rest of the people.

EUCHARIST — The Real Presence of Jesus under the forms of bread and wine.

EUCHARISTIC MEAL — The celebration of the people of God during which the Body and Blood of Jesus is shared.

EXORCISM — The act of driving out an evil spirit.

FORMAL PRAYER — Prayer with definite words and/or actions.

GALILEAN MINISTRY — Jesus' work during most of his public life, performed in the region of Galilee.

GALILEE — The northernmost area of Palestine, home of Jesus.

GENTILE — Anyone who was not a Jew. A nonbeliever.

GOLGOTHA — The name of the place where Christ was crucified. Also called Mount Calvary.

HERESY — An idea or teaching which someone chooses contrary to the teaching of the Christian community.

HYPOCRITE — One who pretends to be holy or virtuous.

IDOLATRY — The worship given to a person or thing which properly belongs to God.

IMMACULATE CONCEPTION — The feast that celebrates the fact that Mary was preserved from original sin from the first moment of her conception.

INCARNATION — The mystery of Jesus, truly God, becoming man.

INFANCY NARRATIVES — The stories of Jesus' birth and the surrounding events as found in Luke and Matthew.

JERUSALEM — The capital of Palestine and center of all Jewish life.

JERUSALEM MINISTRY — Jesus' last couple of weeks, spent working and teaching around the city of Jerusalem.

JESUS — Hebrew name meaning "Yahweh saves."

JEW — One who is a member of the Hebrew people and belongs to the religion which follows the Law of Moses.

JORDAN RIVER — The largest river of Palestine, which flows from Mt. Hermon in the north through the Sea of Galilee to the Dead Sea in the south.

JUDEA — The southern region of Palestine with Jerusaem for its capital.

KINGDOM OF GOD — The reign or authority of God over the hearts and minds of his followers.

LAST JUDGMENT — The final determination of a person's everlasting destiny.

LEPER — Any person with a skin disease (at the time of Jesus).

LITURGICAL PRAYER — The prayer of the community. Religious rites used for public worship.

MARTYR — A person killed for religious beliefs. The word is from the Greek meaning "to witness."

MERCY — A characteristic of God which allows him to love us despite the fact that we have offended him.

MESSIAH — Hebrew word meaning "the anointed one": it came to be applied to the person who would be sent by Yahweh to save his people.

MESSIANISM — The beliefs held by those expecting a Messiah.

MIRACLE — An event, unexplainable by the laws of nature, which indicates divine intervention.

MISSION — The task of each Christian to bring others to know Jesus and his Church. From the Latin meaning "to be sent forth."

MONASTIC LIFE — A manner of living together under a common rule, secluded from the world in order to pursue spiritual perfection in the service of God.

NAZARETH — Small town in Galilee, where Jesus grew up.

ORAL TRADITION — The handing down of information from generation to generation by word of mouth, especially teachings.

PARABLE — A comparison or story from everyday life that helps us understand a deeper truth.

PASSOVER — The special supper celebrated each year by the Jews to commemorate their passage from Egypt to the Promised Land.

PATRIARCHAL FAMILY — A family in which the father rules over everyone in an absolute way.

PENANCE — The sacrament (frequently called reconciliation) in which Jesus heals and forgives us of our sins.

PENTECOST — A feast on the seventh Sunday after Easter commemorating the descent of the Holy Spirit on the Apostles.

PERSECUTION — The harassment or killing of people because of their religious belief, ethnic origin or social outlook. For example, many Christians were persecuted for their belief in Jesus.

PETITION — The act of asking for something.

PHARISEE — (Means separated ones); those who adhered to a strict following of the Law.

PILGRIMAGE — A journey to a shrine for a religious purpose; i.e., for worship, to fulfill a promise, to seek spiritual aid.

PRAISE — In prayer, the act of responding to the supremacy of God.

PRIEST — A member of the Jewish priestly family with certain privileges.

PRIVATE PRAYER — Prayer by oneself.

PROPHET — A person who proclaims a message from God.

PUBLICANS — Tax collectors who worked for the Romans.

RABBI — A teacher. One who usually led the services in the synagogue and answered questions the people would ask.

RELIGION — A body of beliefs and manner of worshiping God.

REPENT — To change one's life, to reform.

RESURRECTION — The physical rising from death by Jesus Christ. The rising again to life of all the human dead before the final judgment.

RITUAL — A form for carrying out religious rites and ceremonies.

SACRAMENT — Action of Christ that gives us a share in the divine life and changes us in some way if our hearts are open to him.

SACRAMENTAL — An object that is blessed by the Church and has some special religious meaning, or acts as a reminder of some religious truth.

SADDUCEES — (From Sadoc, a priest at the time of David); members of the priestly family.

SAMARITANS — A mixed people descended from the Israelites who lived near the city of Sichem. They were rivals of the Jews and were looked down upon by them.

SCANDAL — Bad example in thought, word, or deed.

SCRIBES — Learned men of the Law.

SORROW — The expression of sadness over a deed done.

SPIRIT OF THE LAW — Hidden meaning of the Law.

SPIRITUAL — Refers to those aspects of life which are beyond the physical.

SPONTANEOUS PRAYER — A prayer made up "on the spot."

SYNAGOGUE — A gathering place of the Jewish people for religious services. Used by those Jews unable to get to the Temple.

SYNOPTIC — The Greek word for "looking at together." The term that came to be applied to the Gospels of Matthew, Mark, and Luke.

TEMPLE — An enclosed place of worship; for the Jews, the sacred building in Jerusalem which was the center of all their faith and religion.

TEMPTATION — Enticement to do wrong by promise of pleasure or gain.

THANKSGIVING — The act of gratitude.

THEOLOGY — The study of God and things pertaining to God.

TITHING — The practice of giving one tenth of one's wealth to the support of the Church and care of the poor.

VATICAN — The city within the city of Rome where the pope lives and directs the affairs of the Church.

VIRGIN BIRTH — Jesus being conceived and born in a special manner, without a human father.

ZEALOTS — A political group who sought to drive the Romans out of Israel by force.

Prayers

The Sign of the Cross

In the name of the Father, and of the Son, and of the Holy Spirit. Amen.

The Lord's Prayer

Our Father, who art in heaven, hallowed be thy name; thy kingdom come; thy will be done on earth as it is in heaven. Give us this day our daily bread; and forgive us our trespasses as we forgive those who trespass against us; and lead us not into temptation, but deliver us from evil. Amen.

Glory Be to the Father

Glory be to the Father, and to the Son, and to the Holy Spirit. As it was in the beginning, is now, and ever shall be, world without end. Amen.

Come, Holy Spirit

Come, Holy Spirit, fill the hearts of your faithful, and enkindle in them the fire of your love.

V. Send forth your Spirit, and they shall be created:

R. And you shall renew the face of the earth.

O God, who instructs the hearts of your faithful by the light of your Holy Spirit, grant us by the same Holy Spirit to be truly wise and ever to rejoice in his consolation. Through Christ our Lord. Amen.

Hail Mary

Hail, Mary, full of grace! The Lord is with you. Blessed are you among women, and blessed is the fruit of your womb, Jesus.

Holy Mary, Mother of God, pray for us sinners, now and at the hour of our death. Amen.

The Apostles' Creed

I believe in God, the Father almighty, Creator of heaven and earth; and in Jesus Christ, his only Son, our Lord, who was conceived by the Holy Spirit, born of the Virgin Mary, suffered under Pontius Pilate, was crucified, died, and was buried. He descended into hell; the third day he rose again from the dead. He ascended into heaven and sits at the right hand of God, the Father almighty; from thence he shall come to judge the living and the dead.

I believe in the Holy Spirit, the holy Catholic Church, the communion of saints, the forgiveness of sins, the resurrection of the body, and life everlasting. Amen.

Nicene Creed

We believe in one God, the Father, the Almighty, maker of heaven and earth, of all that is seen and unseen.

We believe in one Lord, Jesus Christ, the only Son of God, eternally begotten of the Father, God from God, Light from Light, true God from true God, begotten, not made, one in Being with the Father.

Through him all things were made. For us men and for our salvation he came down from heaven: by the power of the Holy Spirit he was born of the Virgin Mary, and became man.

For our sake he was crucified under Pontius Pilate; he suffered, died, and was buried. On the third day he rose again in fulfillment of the Scriptures; he ascended into heaven and is seated at the right hand of the Father.

He will come again in glory to judge the living and the dead, and his kingdom will have no end.

We believe in the Holy Spirit, the Lord, the giver of life, who proceeds from the Father and the Son. With the Father and the Son he is worshiped and glorified. He has spoken through the Prophets. We believe in one holy catholic and apostolic Church. We acknowledge one baptism for the forgiveness of sins. We look for the resurrection of the dead, and the life of the world to come. Amen.

Acts of Contrition

My God,
I am sorry for my sins with all my heart.
In choosing to do wrong
and failing to do good,
I have sinned against you
whom I should love above all things.
I firmly intend, with your help,
to do penance,
to sin no more,
and to avoid whatever leads me to sin.
Our Savior, Jesus Christ,
suffered and died for us.
In his name, my God, have mercy.

* * *

Luke 15.18; 18.13
Father, I have sinned against you;
I no longer deserve to be called your son.
Be merciful to me, a sinner.

* * *

Lord Jesus, Son of God, have mercy on me.

Act of Faith

O my God, I firmly believe that you are one God in three divine Persons, Father, Son, and Holy Spirit. I believe in Jesus Christ, your Son, who became man and died for our sins, and who will come to judge the living and the dead. I believe these and all the truths which the holy Catholic Church teaches, because you have revealed them, who cannot deceive or be deceived.

Act of Hope

O my God, trusting in your infinite goodness and promises, I hope to obtain the pardon of my sins, the help of your grace, and life everlasting, through the merits of Jesus Christ, my Lord and my Redeemer.

Act of Love

O my God, I love you above all things with my whole heart and soul, because you are all-good and worthy of all my love. I love my neighbor as myself for the love of you. I forgive all who have injured me, and I ask pardon of all whom I have injured.

The Mysteries of the Rosary

The Joyful Mysteries

1. The Annunciation.
2. The Visitation.
3. The Birth of our Lord.
4. The Presentation in the Temple.
5. The Finding of the Child Jesus in the Temple.

The Sorrowful Mysteries

1. The Agony in the Garden.
2. The Scourging at the Pillar.
3. The Crowning with Thorns.
4. The Carrying of the Cross.
5. The Crucifixion.

The Glorious Mysteries

1. The Resurrection.
2. The Ascension.
3. The Descent of the Holy Spirit.
4. The Assumption.
5. The Crowning of the Blessed Virgin Mary.

Morning Prayer

Father, help us through this day that it may be spent in your service. In all our thoughts, words, and actions may we do your will faithfully for love of you and our brothers and sisters. Amen.

Evening Prayer

Watch over us, Lord, this night. By your strength may we rise at daybreak to rejoice in the resurrection of Christ, your Son, who lives and reigns for ever and ever. Amen.

Grace Before Meals

Bless us, O Lord, and these your gifts which we are about to receive from your bounty, through Christ our Lord. Amen.

Grace After Meals

We give you thanks, O Lord, for all the graces and benefits we have received from your bounty, through Christ our Lord. Amen.

(May the souls of the faithful departed, through the mercy of God, rest in peace. Amen.)

Prayer for Peace
(Attributed to St. Francis of Assisi)

Lord, make me an instrument of your peace.
Where there is hatred, let me sow love;
where there is injury, pardon;
where there is discord, unity;
where there is doubt, faith;
where there is despair, hope;

where there is darkness, light;
where there is sadness, joy.
O divine master,
grant that I may not so much
seek to be consoled as to console;
to be understood as to understand;
to be loved as to love.
For it is in giving that we receive;
it is in pardoning that we are pardoned;
and it is in dying that we are born to
eternal life.
Amen.

Hail, Holy Queen

Hail, Holy Queen,
Mother of Mercy:
Hail, our life, our sweetness,
and our hope:
To you do we cry,
poor banished children of Eve;
to you do we send up our sighs,
mourning and weeping
in this valley of tears.
Turn, then, most gracious advocate,
your eyes of mercy toward us;
and after this, our exile,
show unto us
the blessed fruit of your womb, Jesus.
O clement, O loving,
O sweet Virgin Mary.
Amen.

The Memorare

Remember, O most gracious Virgin
Mary,
that never was it known
that anyone who fled to your
protection,
implored your help,
or sought your intercession
was left unaided.
Inspired by this confidence,
I fly to you,
O virgin of virgins, my mother.
To you I come,
before you I stand,
sinful and sorrowful.
O Mother of the Word Incarnate,
do not ignore my petitions,
but in your mercy
hear and pray for me.
Amen.

Angelus
(Traditionally prayed from Pentecost to Easter;
otherwise the Regina Caeli prayer is substituted.)

The angel of the Lord declared unto Mary:
And she conceived of the Holy Spirit.
Hail Mary . . .
Behold the handmaid of the Lord:
Be it done to me according to thy word.
Hail Mary . . .
And the Word was made flesh:
And dwelt among us.
Hail Mary . . .
Pray for us, O holy Mother of God:
That we may be made worthy
of the promises of Christ.
Pour forth, we beseech thee, O Lord,
thy grace into our hearts,
that we, to whom the Incarnation
of Christ, thy Son,
was made known by the message
of an angel,
may, by his Passion and Cross,
be brought to the glory
of his resurrection.
Through the same Christ our Lord.
Amen.

Regina Caeli — 'Queen of Heaven'

(Traditionally prayed in place of the Angelus from Easter Sunday to the Friday after Pentecost.)

O Queen of Heaven, rejoice;
alleluia!
For he whom you did merit to bear —
alleluia!
Has risen as he said:
alleluia!
Pray for us to God;
alleluia!
V. Rejoice and be glad, O Virgin Mary;
alleluia!
R. For the Lord has risen indeed;
alleluia!

O God, who gave joy to the world
Through the resurrection of your Son,
our Lord Jesus Christ:
grant that we may obtain,
through his Virgin Mother, Mary,
the joys of everlasting life.
Through the same Christ our Lord.
Amen.

The Magnificat

My soul proclaims the greatness of the Lord,
my spirit rejoices in God my Savior
for he has looked with favor on his lowly servant.
From this day all generations will call me blessed:
the Almighty has done great things for me,
and holy is his Name.
He has mercy on those who fear him
in every generation.
He has shown the strength of his arm,
he has scattered the proud in their conceit.
He has cast down the mighty from their thrones,
and has lifted up the lowly.
He has filled the hungry with good things,
and the rich he has sent away empty.
He has come to the help of his servant Israel
for he has remembered his promise of mercy,
the promise he made to our fathers,
to Abraham and his children forever.

Litany of the Blessed Virgin

Lord, have mercy.
Christ, have mercy.
Lord, have mercy.
Christ, hear us.
Christ, graciously hear us.
God, the Father of heaven:
Have mercy on us.
God, the Son, redeemer of the world:
Have mercy on us.
God, the Holy Spirit:
Have mercy on us.
Holy Trinity, one God:
Have mercy on us.
Holy Mary:
Pray for us.
Holy Mother of God:
Holy virgin of virgins:
Mother of Christ:
Mother of divine grace:
Mother most holy:
Mother most chaste:
Mother inviolate:
Mother undefiled:
Mother most amiable:

Mother most admirable:
Mother of good counsel:
Mother of our Creator:
Mother of our Savior:
Virgin most prudent:
Virgin most venerable:
Virgin most renowned:
Virgin most powerful:
Virgin most merciful:
Virgin most faithful:
Mirror of Justice:
Seat of Wisdom:
Cause of our joy:
Spiritual Vessel:
Vessel of Honor:
Singular vessel of devotion:
Mystical Rose:
Tower of David:
Tower of Ivory:
House of Gold:
Ark of the Covenant:
Gate of Heaven:
Morning Star:
Health of the sick:
Refuge of sinners:
Comforter of the afflicted:
Help of Christians:
Queen of angels:
Queen of patriarchs:
Queen of prophets:
Queen of apostles:
Queen of martyrs:
Queen of confessors:
Queen of virgins:
Queen of all saints:
Queen conceived without original sin:
Queen assumed into heaven:
Queen of the holy Rosary:
Queen of peace:
Lamb of God,
who take away the sins of the world:
Spare us, O Lord.
Lamb of God,
who take away the sins of the world:
Graciously hear us, O Lord.
Lamb of God,
who take away the sins of the world:
Have mercy on us.
Pray for us, O holy Mother of God:
that we may be made worthy of the promises of Christ.

Grant, we beseech you, O Lord God, that we your servants may enjoy lasting health of mind and body, and by the intercession of the Blessed Virgin Mary, be delivered from present sorrow and enter into the joy of eternal happiness. We ask this through the merits of Jesus Christ, our Lord. Amen.

Litany of the Holy Name of Jesus

Lord, have mercy on us.
Christ, have mercy on us.
Lord, have mercy on us.
Christ, hear us.
Christ, graciously hear us.
God the Father of heaven:
Have mercy on us.
God the Son, Redeemer of the world:
God the Holy Spirit:
Holy Trinity, one God:
Jesus, Son of the Living God:
Jesus, splendor of the Father:
Jesus, brightness of eternal light:
Jesus, King of Glory:
Jesus, Sun of Justice:
Jesus, Son of the Virgin Mary:
Jesus, most amiable:
Jesus, most admirable:
Jesus, mighty God:

Jesus, Father of the world to come:
Jesus, Angel of great counsel:
Jesus, most powerful:
Jesus, most patient:
Jesus, most obedient:
Jesus, meek and humble of heart:
Jesus, lover of chastity:
Jesus, lover of us:
Jesus, God of Peace:
Jesus, Author of Life:
Jesus, model of virtues:
Jesus, zealous for souls:
Jesus, our God:
Jesus, our refuge:
Jesus, Father of the poor:
Jesus, treasure of the faithful:
Jesus, Good Shepherd:
Jesus, true Light:
Jesus, eternal wisdom:
Jesus, infinite goodness:
Jesus, our way and our life:
Jesus, joy of angels:
Jesus, King of Patriarchs:
Jesus, Master of the Apostles:
Jesus, teacher of the evangelists:
Jesus, strength of martyrs:
Jesus, light of confessors:
Jesus purity of virgins:
Jesus, crown of all saints: —

Be merciful: *Spare us, O Jesus.*
Be merciful: *Graciously hear us, O Jesus.*

From all evil: *Jesus, deliver us.*
From all sin:
From thy wrath:
From the snares of the devil:
From the spirit of fornication:
From everlasting death:
From neglect of thy inspirations:

Through the mystery of thy Incarnation:
Through thy Nativity:
Through thy infancy:
Through thy most divine life:
Through thy labors:
Through thy agony and passion:
Through thy cross and dereliction:
Through thy weariness and faintness:
Through thy death and burial:
Through thy Resurrection:
Through thy Ascension:
Through thy joys:
Through thy glory:
Through thy institution of the Blessed Sacrament: —

Lamb of God,
who take away the sins of the world:
Spare us, O Jesus.
Lamb of God,
who take away the sins of the world:
Graciously hear us, O Jesus.
Lamb of God,
who take away the sins of the world:
Have mercy on us, O Jesus.
Jesus, hear us.
Jesus, graciously hear us.
We will praise thee, O God.
And we will call upon thy name.

O Lord Jesus Christ, who has said, "Ask and you shall receive; seek and you shall find; knock and it shall be opened unto you," grant, we beseech thee, that we may love thee with a whole heart, in our words and in our work, and never cease to praise thy name.
Amen.

Things to Know

The Ten Commandments
(Exodus 20.1-17; Deuteronomy 5.6-21)

1. I, the Lord, am your God; you shall not have other gods besides me.
2. You shall not take the name of the Lord, your God, in vain.
3. Remember to keep holy the sabbath day.
4. Honor your father and your mother.
5. You shall not kill.
6. You shall not commit adultery.
7. You shall not steal.
8. You shall not bear false witness against your neighbor.
9. You shall not covet your neighbor's wife.
10. You shall not covet anything that belongs to your neighbor.

The Great Commandments
(Matthew 22.37-40; Mark 12.29-31; Luke 10.27)

1. You shall love the Lord your God with your whole heart, with your whole soul, and with all your mind.
2. You shall love your neighbor as yourself.

The Beatitudes
(Matthew 5.3-10)

1. How blest are the poor in spirit: the reign of God is theirs.
2. Blest too are the sorrowing; they shall be consoled.
3. [Blest are the lowly; they shall inherit the land.]
4. Blest are they who hunger and thirst for holiness; they shall have their fill.
5. Blest are they who show mercy; mercy shall be theirs.
6. Blest are the single-hearted for they shall see God.
7. Blest too are the peacemakers; they shall be called sons of God.
8. Blest are those persecuted for holiness' sake; the reign of God is theirs.

Corporal Works of Mercy

To feed the hungry.
To give drink to the thirsty.
To clothe the naked.
To shelter the homeless.
To visit the sick.
To ransom the captive.
To bury the dead.

Spiritual Works of Mercy

To instruct the ignorant.
To counsel the doubtful.
To admonish sinners.
To bear wrongs patiently.
To forgive offenses.
To comfort the afflicted.
To pray for the living and the dead.

Seven Sacraments

Baptism.
Confirmation.
Eucharist.
Penance.
Anointing of the Sick.
Holy Orders.
Matrimony.

Holy Days of Obligation (United States)

- Christmas, the Nativity of Jesus — December 25.
- Solemnity of Mary the Mother of God — January 1.
- Ascension of the Lord — Movable Feast.
- Assumption of the Blessed Virgin Mary — August 15.
- All Saints' Day — November 1.
- Immaculate Conception of the Blessed Virgin Mary — December 8.

Stations of the Cross

1. Jesus is condemned to death.
2. Jesus takes up the cross.
3. Jesus falls the first time.
4. Jesus meets his blessed Mother.
5. Simon helps Jesus to carry the cross.
6. Veronica wipes the face of Jesus.
7. Jesus falls the second time.
8. Jesus comforts the women of Jerusalem.
9. Jesus falls the third time.
10. Jesus is stripped of his garments.
11. Jesus is nailed to the cross.
12. Jesus dies upon the cross.
13. Jesus' body is taken down from the cross.
14. Jesus' body is laid in the tomb.
15. *(optional)* Jesus is raised to life.

Precepts of the Church

- Assist at Mass on Sundays and holy days of obligation.
- Fast and abstain on the days appointed.
- Confess sins at least once a year.
- Receive Holy Communion during the Easter season.
- Contribute to the support of the Church.
- Observe the laws of the Church concerning marriage.